BELL IN CAMPO

THE SOCIABLE COMPANIONS

BELL IN CAMPO

THE SOCIABLE COMPANIONS

Margaret Cavendish

edited by Alexandra G. Bennett

broadview literary texts

National Library of Canada Cataloguing in Publication Data
Newcastle, Margaret Cavendish, Duchess of, 1624?-1674
   Bell in Campo, and, The sociable companions
(Broadview literacy texts)
Includes bibliographical references.
ISBN 1-55111-287-6

1. Newcastle, Margaret Cavendish, Duchess of, 1624?-1674. Bell in Campo.
2. Newcastle, Margaret Cavendish, Duchess of, 1624?-1674. Sociable companions.
3. Newcastle, Margaret Cavendish, Duchess of, 1624?-1674—Criticism and interpretation. 4. Great Britain—Civil War, 1642-1649. I. Bennett, Alexandra G., 1970- II. Title. III. Title: Sociable companions. IV. Series.

PR3605.N2A6 2002   822'.4   C2001-903157-2

Broadview Press Ltd. is an independent, international publishing house, incorporated in 1985.

North America:
P.O. Box 1243, Peterborough, Ontario, Canada K9J 7H5
3576 California Road, Orchard Park, NY 14127
TEL: (705) 743-8990; FAX: (705) 743-8353;
E-MAIL: customerservice@broadviewpress.com

United Kingdom:
Thomas Lyster Ltd
Unit 9, Ormskirk Industrial Park
Old Boundary Way, Burscough Road
Ormskirk, Lancashire L39 2YW
TEL: (01695) 575112; FAX: (01695) 570120; E-mail: books@tlyster.co.uk

Australia:
St. Clair Press, P.O. Box 287, Rozelle, NSW 2039
TEL: (02) 818-1942; FAX: (02) 418-1923

www.broadviewpress.com

Broadview Press gratefully acknowledges the financial support of the Book Publishing Industry Development Program, Ministry of Canadian Heritage, Government of Canada.

Broadview Press is grateful to Professor Eugene Benson and to Professor L. W. Conolly for advice on editorial matters for the Broadview Literary Texts series.

Text design and composition by George Kirkpatrick
PRINTED IN CANADA

Contents

Acknowledgements

I am indebted to several colleagues, particularly Anne Shaver, Gweno Williams, Sophie Tomlinson, and Stephen Clucas, who have been generous in sharing their work and ideas in various forums, as well as to Mical Moser at Broadview Press for thinking that the vague suggestion I made for an edition of Cavendish plays three years ago was a good idea. I am also grateful to Mrs. Mary Clapinson, Keeper of Special Collections and Western Manuscripts at the Bodleian Library, Oxford, for permission to quote from the Bodleian's manuscript collections. Most of all, I would like to thank my father, Greg Bennett, for his help in transcribing *The Sociable Companions* and for clarifying several obscure classical references therein; my mother, Gaynor Bennett, for her patience and continued interest in what may have seemed like an endless project; and both of my parents together for their boundless support.

Introduction

Life, Career, and Reputation

Among English women writers prior to Aphra Behn, few have become so provocative to scholars in the past twenty years as Margaret Cavendish, Duchess of Newcastle. Proto-feminist, semi-scientist, philosopher, poet, playwright, fantasist—her seemingly endless inventiveness has provided modern readers with a wealth of material. A staunch Royalist and lady-in-waiting to Queen Henrietta Maria during the years of the English Civil War, she lived for sixteen years in exile, married a man considerably higher in the social scale than herself despite the disapproval of her royal mistress, and ultimately became famous (or infamous) for her self-designed clothing, for her flamboyant personal style, and (not least) for her prolific writing and publishing.

Unlike those of many of the women who took up the pen during the seventeenth century, Cavendish's personal history is remarkably well detailed, thanks to her having composed *A True Relation of My Birth, Breeding, and Life*, an autobiography appended to the first edition of her collected stories and poems, *Natures Pictures Drawn by Fancies Pencil to the Life* (1656). According to this account, the earliest years of her life do not appear to have been presciently fraught with excitement. Born in 1623, Margaret Lucas was the youngest of eight children. Her father, Thomas Lucas of St. John's, near Colchester, was a gentleman who had to go into exile temporarily after killing a man in a duel. He died during Margaret's infancy, leaving her mother, Elizabeth Lucas, daughter of John Leighton, gentleman of London, to raise her three sons and five daughters herself. The Lucas girls were accordingly given a basic education in the skills expected of seventeenth-century gentlewomen: reading, writing, sewing, music, and dancing, while their mother enjoyed indulging their "honest pleasures, and harmless delights" with the proceeds from the substantial family estate.[1] Margaret writes that she and her siblings "were bred virtuously, modestly, civilly, honourably, and on honest principles: as for plenty, we had not only, for necessity, convenience, and decency, but for delight and pleasure to a superfluity; 'tis true, we did not riot, but we lived orderly" and in apparently mutual concord throughout her childhood.[2]

By her late teens, however, Margaret was determined to become a lady-in-waiting at the court of Queen Henrietta Maria, who had removed herself to Oxford at the outset of the struggles that had turned into civil war by 1642. Despite the fears of her mother and misgivings of her siblings, she moved to the Queen's court in 1643. Almost immediately, her brothers' and sisters' reservations about the possible consequences of her inexperience of the world outside of their home proved justified: terrified that she might inadvertently say or do something immodest, Margaret was so timid she barely opened her mouth in her new surroundings. Not surprisingly, such shyness earned her the reputation of a fool in a world of courtiers and patrons where wit ruled supreme. At the same time, the idyllic environment of her childhood was devastated as her mother and brothers, staunch Royalists all, were "sequestered from their estates, and plundered of all their goods" by the Parliamentary government.[3] Faced with familial ruin amid the tempestuous life of a royal servant, she must have felt adrift in more ways than one when she took ship for exile in France with the rest of the Queen's household in 1644.

Rescue from at least some of her miseries, however, was to come in Paris, where she met William Cavendish, then Marquis (later Earl and Duke) of Newcastle. Unlike his fellow courtiers, who ignored or mocked the bashful girl in their midst, Newcastle took a fancy to her, writing her flirtatious letters and poems and ultimately falling in love with her. His first wife having recently died, the Marquis proposed to the deeply

---

1   *A True Relation of My Birth, Breeding, and Life*, as appended to *Natures Pictures Drawn by Fancies Pencil to the Life* (London: 1656), 369. It is interesting to note that *A True Relation* was omitted from the second edition of *Natures Pictures* in 1671.
2   *A True Relation*, 398.
3   *A True Relation*, 374.

smitten lady-in-waiting; she married him in 1645 despite the disapprobation of the Queen, who felt that the differences of thirty years and several social ranks between them were too much of an impediment to be overcome easily. The couple lived in Paris and then in Antwerp during the years of the English Interregnum; since Newcastle's estates, like those of the Lucas family, had been appropriated and looted by the Parliamentary army, they were forced like so many other exiled gentry to live mostly on credit, with occasional monetary relief smuggled over from home.

This precarious financial situation ultimately gave rise to Margaret Cavendish's public literary career. In 1653, she returned temporarily to England in an attempt to retrieve her husband's sequestered lands and to raise some money to alleviate the costs of living on the Continent. Though the trip was financially unsuccessful (her shyness once again entrapped her tongue, rendering her unable even to address the Parliamentary committee meeting she attended), her publication of *Poems and Fancies* and *Philosophicall Fancies* that year gained her the attention of some members of the London reading public. Hungry for fame, from that point onwards she continued to produce—and, unusually, to publish—her works, writing both while in exile and once she returned to England after the Restoration of Charles II in 1660. She and her husband took up residence at his family home of Welbeck, with the notable exception of her visit to London in 1667, during which she became the first woman ever to be invited to visit a session of the recently-founded Royal Society. She managed to compose fourteen printed folio volumes of generically diverse writings by the time of her death in 1673; fittingly, the inscription on the tomb she shares with her husband in Westminster Abbey proclaims that "This Dutches was a wise, wittie, and Learned Lady, which her many Bookes do well testifie."

Margaret Cavendish was one of the most prolific writers of any genre or gender in the seventeenth century, expounding her views and extending her creative reach into prose fiction, poetry, plays, scientific and philosophical treatises, biography, autobiography, orations, and letters. Moreover, she was one of the first authors (and certainly the first woman) to avail herself actively of the wide public circulation provided by the medium of print. Not only did she present copies of all of her works to prominent institutions, including the universities of Oxford and Cambridge, but she addressed herself specifically to her readers in each volume of her writing, frequently responded to comments or criticisms in subsequent works, and ultimately succeeded in becoming a publishing innovator in a number of original genres.

However, it can be difficult to decide whether "fame" or "infamy" is the appropriate term to apply to the end results of her life and literary career. Certainly her contemporaries were far from unanimously admiring of her authorial achievements or her personal style, as the unattributed nickname "Mad Madge" suggests. In his famous diary, Samuel Pepys dismissed her as "a mad, conceited, ridiculous woman," and described her 1667 outings in London's Hyde Park as the ultimate in social spectacle: "That which we and almost all went for was to see my Lady Newcastle" in her startling coach of black trimmed with silver, mobbed by the gaping crowds to such an extent "that nobody could come near her."[1] On April 13, 1667, Charles North wrote to his father that

> Dutchess Newcastle is all yᵉ pageant now discoursed on: Her brests all laid out to view in a play house with scarlett trimd nipples. Her intrado was incognito else a triumphall chariott with 12 horses & another with 8 white bulls was prepard. But I know not what hindred. But at court My Lᵈ Chamberlain forbids her liveries wearing affected Velvet caps like yᵉ King's footmen.[2]

Such contemporary comment was not restricted to Cavendish's fashion sense, but was particularly vitriolic in relation to her publications. In describing her first impressions of the Duchess,

---

1   Samuel Pepys, *The Diary of Samuel Pepys*, ed. Robert Latham and William Matthews, 11 vols. (London: G. Bell and Sons, 1974), 9:123, 8:196.
2   Thomas, Lord North, *Correspondence of the Fourth Lord North*, Oxford, Bodleian Library, MS. North c. 4.

for instance, Mary Evelyn drew deliberate and scathing parallels between Cavendish's life and her works:

> I was surprised to find so much extravagancy and vanity in any person not confined within four walls. Her habit peculiar, fantastical....Her mien surpasses the imagination of poets, or the descriptions of a romance heroine's greatness: her gracious bows, seasonable nods, courteous stretching out of her hands, twinkling of her eyes, and various gestures of approbation, show what may be expected from her discourse, which is as airy, empty, whimsical and rambling as her books.[1]

Upon the publication of *Poems and Fancies* in 1653, Dorothy Osborne wrote to her lover William Temple:

> [L]et mee aske you if you have seen a book of Poems newly come out, made by my Lady New Castle. for God sake if you meet with it send it mee, they say tis ten times more Extravagant then her dresse. Sure the poore woman is a little distracted, she could never be soe rediculous else as to venture at writeing book's and in verse too, If I should not sleep this fortnight I should not come to that.[2]

Most cruelly, an anonymous lampoon proclaimed her to be "Welbeck's illustrious whore," though there is absolutely no evidence to suggest that Cavendish was anything of the kind.[3] Nevertheless, the explicit links drawn by contemporary commentators between a woman's writing and her sexuality (as most clearly evinced by the later public career of Aphra Behn), as well as the dominant image of the Duchess possessing an imagination run riot, persisted.

Yet it is also important to note that despite the censure of

---

1 Mary Evelyn, letter to John Evelyn reprinted in *The Diary of John Evelyn*, ed. E.S. de Beer, 6 vols. (Oxford: Clarendon Press, 1857), 8.

2 Dorothy Osborne, *The Letters from Dorothy Osborne to Sir William Temple*, ed. G.C. Moore Smith (Oxford: Clarendon Press, 1928), 37.

3 Douglas Grant, *Margaret the First* (London: Rupert Hart-Davis 1957), 199.

some critics, Cavendish's writing was anything but dismissed during the seventeenth century. Readers may have scoffed at both her and her authorship, but they also begged for copies of her books, as Osborne's letter demonstrates. Pepys described her 1667 biography of William Cavendish as "ridiculous" and proof that her husband was "an asse to suffer her to write what she writes to him and of him," but stayed up all night to read the copy a friend had lent to his wife.[1] Others were more overtly appreciative: three years after her death, a commemorative volume of letters and poems was published in her honour, including multiple letters from the Oxford and Cambridge colleges to which she had submitted her works and contributions from writers such as Thomas Shadwell and Thomas Hobbes.[2] The Duke of Newcastle, a poet and playwright in his own right, actively encouraged his wife's writing, and even (as is the case in *Bell in Campo*) contributed poems and songs of his own to her works. Cavendish's writing may not be conventional, particularly by modern standards, but nor is it trifling.

Bell in Campo, *The Sociable Companions*, and the English Civil War

Cavendish composed two complete folio volumes of plays: *Playes Written by the Thrice Noble, Illustrious, and Excellent Princess, the Lady Marchioness of Newcastle* (London, 1662), from whence *Bell in Campo* is taken, and *Plays Never Before Printed* (London, 1668), in which *The Sociable Companions* is found. Though the specific dates of composition for the individual plays in each collection are not given, the subject material and treatment of it in the plays presented here suggest that *Bell in Campo* was almost certainly written during the years of the Civil War, while *The Sociable Companions* was probably written not long after the Restoration. Though Cavendish was a staunch Royalist in her beliefs, she was not averse to commenting pointedly upon the political and cultural environments

---

1   *Diary of Samuel Pepys*, 9:123.
2   *Letters and Poems in Honour of the Incomparable Princess, Margaret, Duchess of Newcastle*. London: 1676.

which shaped her dramatic works. Both plays deal with the circumstances of war, its effects, and its aftermath, particularly in relation to women and their social roles.

At first glance, the plot and characters of *Bell in Campo* would appear to be entirely fictional, if not outright allegorical: the dastardly Kingdom of Faction declares war on the virtuous Kingdom of Reformation (like Ben Jonson and numerous other playwrights before her, Cavendish was prone to giving her characters names indicative of their natures). As the impeccable Lord General prepares to lead the Reformation army against the invaders, his wife, Lady Victoria, announces her firm intention to accompany him. He objects, but is eventually won over by her arguments, and a number of wives join their husbands on the journey. Once they reach the battlefield, the men insist upon placing the women in a nearby town out of both harm's and mischief's way. Outraged, the women form an army of their own, under strict regulations and led by Lady Victoria. Ultimately, the female army sweeps into a close-fought battle and rescues the men from danger, leading to an utter rout of the Faction forces. After acknowledging the women's pivotal role in the victory, the men hail Lady Victoria as a national heroine and give the army a triumphant processional into the nation's capital, where a proclamation giving all women domestic and social rights is read aloud and a statue is raised of the female general.

It would be easy to see the play as an elaborate fantasy of agency for a supporter of the royal cause by an author who could cast herself in the lead role: William Cavendish had been a general in the royal army before his exile upon a disastrous defeat at Marston Moor in 1644, and his wife's deep love for him could certainly make itself manifest in a vision of rescuing him from peril. Such a reading would be consistent with years of interpretation of the Duchess's works as the effusive outpourings of a vivid fantasy life. But such a reading ignores the fact that women actually did fight for both sides in the English Civil War, either by making no secret at all of their gender (as in the case of Lady Ann Cunningham, a Scots noblewoman who refused to acquiesce to royal authority during the 1630s) or by passing themselves off as men and fighting alongside kins-men or lovers (as did one Ann Dimack in the Parliamentary army). Contemporary accounts of these women are given in Appendix C, as are copies of documents highlighting the mili-tary roles assumed by Cavendish's mistress, Queen Henrietta Maria, who styled herself "her she-majesty generalissima" in a letter to her husband (see Appendix D). At the same time, it is important to note that the 'fantasy' of the play is not only embodied in its depiction of victorious women, but also in the eventual triumph of the royal Kingdom of Reformation itself over its adversaries: as the letters from Edward Norgate to Robert Read in Appendix C indicate, the conduct of the actu-al royal army under Charles I and his generals was far from the model of discipline and determination portrayed in the play-text. William Cavendish not only endured social slights from his fellow commanders, but had to deal with a badly-trained, ill-equipped army of reluctant soldiers: a far cry from his wife's dramatization of the Lord General's virtues and his followers' loyalty. In writing such a highly idealized portrait, Cavendish indulged in specifically Royalist wishful thinking within the bounds of her allegorical framework.

Yet *Bell in Campo* is not simply limited to the rollicking story of a female army. The play's subplots, in which the options and actions of a contrasting pair of gentlewomen widowed early in the war are explored, give a fuller account of the effects of war. While Madam Jantil retires into utter seclusion to mourn the death of her husband (much as Cavendish describes the reac-tion of her mother to her father's death in her autobiography, Appendix A), Madam Passionate grieves extravagantly for a short while but quickly perks up again once several young men come courting. In choosing the youngest and most attractive of all the fortune-hunters, though, she becomes vulnerable and exploited by her careless new spouse and lives to regret her decision. The play as a whole thus provides a richly complex exploration of the transformed conditions brought on by civil strife.

The Sociable Companions forms a fitting sequel to *Bell in Campo*, for it takes as its subject what happens once the war is finally over. The Restoration having been effected, the Royalist army is disbanded and all the gallant Cavaliers must now face the new realities of their penniless existences. Not only are the erstwhile soldiers, already stripped of their familial lands and fortunes, left without viable occupations, but their sisters find themselves to be poor candidates on the marriage market due to their poverty. In a shorter and more tightly composed play than her earlier effort, Cavendish creates three witty women who are determined to gain themselves wealthy husbands through their own ingenuity and a striking diversity of plots. Her observations on contemporary postwar life, including the fact that all the money in town is now concentrated in the hands of lawyers (hired by desperate Cavaliers to get their ancestral lands back), usurers (who made a tidy profit loaning money to the returnees), and doctors (to whom the idle ex-soldiers turned to cure the various venereal diseases brought on by popular female entertainment), are wryly perceptive. As *Bell in Campo* demonstrates the harshness of fortune-hunting marriages from the woman's perspective, *The Sociable Companions* takes a comic view of the practice: not only do the women here succeed in winning the hearts and bankrolls of their new husbands, but one of the Cavaliers manages to wed a rich widow in part through the employment of one of his cross-dressed colleagues. At the same time, Cavendish also sets out the travails of Prudence, a wealthy and witty gentlewoman who must wade through a tide of impertinent and importunate suitors to find a suitable mate. Prudence's final oration to the crowd of outraged unsuccessful candidates is a delightful putdown of all the romantic ideals commonly celebrated in early Restoration drama.

Neither *Bell in Campo* nor *The Sociable Companions* was ever staged during Cavendish's lifetime; indeed, Cavendish herself wrote in one of the many prefaces to her 1662 collection that she had intended her plays to be read rather than acted. However, modern performances of both plays have taken or will soon take place: *The Sociable Companions* was performed under its secondary title (*The Female Wits*) for three weeks at the Canal Café Theatre, Little Venice, London, in January 1995, while a future production of *Bell in Campo* is currently being planned in York.[1] Neither of these texts has been republished until the twentieth century: *The Sociable Companions* was transcribed and edited by Amanda Holton for the Seventeenth Century Press in 1996, and *Bell in Campo* is one of several plays in a collection edited by Anne Shaver for Johns Hopkins University Press in 1999.

Appendices

The appendices are intended to provide background material in order to set both *Bell in Campo* and *The Sociable Companions* in some of their historical and intellectual contexts. Appendix A gives an account of Margaret Cavendish's life and literary career through selections from her own autobiography, originally appended to *Natures Pictures* in 1656 and republished since then as an appendix to the biography she published of her husband. The excerpts printed here paint a vivid portrait of the author and of her development as a thinker and an artist during the tumultuous years of the English civil war. Appendix B follows in providing some of Cavendish's specific thoughts on the nature and purposes of plays themselves; unlike our modern habits of studying drama, Cavendish believed that reading aloud constituted a valid and important performance of her plays, and gave specific instructions on how to read the works effectively. For her, the writing of plays was an endeavour with particular personal resonances.

The implications of Cavendish's works range far beyond the autobiographical, however. The two parts of Appendix C are eyewitness accounts of the involvement of women in the fighting of the civil war, and suggest some of the realities Cavendish may have referred to in crafting the "Amazon Army" of *Bell in Campo*. Certainly, the courageous Lady Victoria may well have

---

1   Margaret Cavendish, *The Female Wits*, dir. George Pensotti, adapt. Judith Peacock, Canal Café Theatre, London, January 1995. I am grateful to Stephen Clucas for providing me with this information, and to Gweno Williams for informing me of her imminent work on *Bell in Campo* at the University College of Ripon and York St. John.

been modeled on the actions of Queen Henrietta Maria in leading Royalist forces successfully back to her husband's waiting armies in 1643, as the Queen's letters to Charles I from that period and the later recollections of her friend Françoise de Motteville in Appendix D indicate. By contrast, the consistent focus on the rapacious marriage market in *The Sociable Companions* finds a number of echoes in the (occasionally radical, and often pointed) ideas about marriage Cavendish expressed in another of her works, the *CCXI Sociable Letters* of 1664. As the selections provided in Appendix E show, Cavendish was a sharp-eyed observer of the social mores of her time; her desire to dramatize and to publish some of what she noted reveals her awareness of both drama and print as forums for public commentary.

Margaret Cavendish, Duchess of Newcastle: A Brief Chronology[1]

1593   William Cavendish born.

1618   William Cavendish marries Elizabeth Howard.

1623   Margaret Lucas born, the youngest of eight children, to Thomas Lucas and Elizabeth Leighton in St. John's, near Colchester, Essex.

1625   Death of Thomas Lucas. Accession of Charles I. Marriage of Charles I to Henrietta Maria of France.

1633   William Cavendish commissions Ben Jonson to write the masque *The Kings Entertainment at Welbeck* for an impending royal visit to his estate at Welbeck, Nottinghamshire.

1634   William Cavendish commissions another Jonson masque, *Love's Welcome at Bolsover,* for a royal visit to his estate at Bolsover Castle, Nottinghamshire.

1637   Charles I attempts to impose English liturgy on Scotland by royal decree. His edict is greeted with violence and the outbreak of the Covenanter rebellion in Scotland.

1640   First meeting of the so-called Long Parliament (November 3, 1640-March 16, 1660) in response to the intensified growth of political and religious unrest in England.

1642   Outbreak of the English Civil War (1642-1660). Public theatres closed.

1643   William Cavendish, Earl of Newcastle, created Marquis. William Cavendish's first wife, Elizabeth, dies. Margaret Lucas becomes a maid of honour at the court of Queen Henrietta Maria. Henrietta Maria visits France and is attacked upon her return, managing to bring reinforcements for the royal troops in rejoining her husband.

---

1   Further biographical details are available in Grant 1957, Jones 1988, and Mendelson 1987. For more details of William Cavendish's dramatic works, see Randall 1995.

1644   Battle of Marston Moor, in which the Royalist forces led by William Cavendish are thoroughly routed by the Parliamentarians. William Cavendish flees into exile in France. Queen Henrietta Maria and her court take refuge in France.

1645   William Cavendish marries Margaret Lucas in December, despite the disapproval of the Queen.

1647   Margaret Cavendish's mother, sister Mary, and niece die of natural causes.

1648   Margaret Cavendish's brother Sir Charles Lucas executed under martial law. Lucas family tomb broken open.

1649   Execution of Charles I. William Cavendish declared a traitor and enemy to the English government, and his estates confiscated. His daughters by his first marriage, Jane, Elizabeth, and Frances, live under house arrest at his family home. William Cavendish publishes two plays: *The Country Captain* and *The Varietie*.

1651   Margaret Cavendish travels to England to attempt to petition Parliament to release income from her husband's estates, but is too bashful to speak in public before the committee. Her petition is denied.

1653   Margaret Cavendish returns to Antwerp, where she and her husband live in exile. Publication of her first books: *Poems and Fancies* and *Philosophical Fancies*.

1655   Publication of *The Worlds Olio* and *Philosophical and Physical Opinions*.

1656   Publication of *Natures Pictures Drawn by Fancy's Pencil to the Life*, which includes the autobiographical account "A True Relation of my Birth, Breeding, and Life."

1658   Publication of William Cavendish's *La Méthode Nouvelle et Invention Extraordinaire de dresser les Chevaux*.

c.1658 William Cavendish writes the play *A Pleasante & Merye Humor off a Roge*.

1660   Charles I restored to the English throne. The Cavendishes return to England to live at Welbeck,

Nottinghamshire. Public theatres reopen. William Cavendish composes a masque, *The King's Entertainment*, for a possible royal visit.

1662 Publication of *Playes* and *Orations of Divers Sorts*. Royal edict proclaims that henceforth all female parts onstage in England must be performed by women, rather than the pre-war boy actors.

1664 Publication of *Philosophical Letters* and *CCXI Sociable Letters*.

1665 William Cavendish created Duke of Newcastle.

1666 Publication of *Observations upon Experimental Philosophy* and *The Description of a New World, called the Blazing World*.

1667 Margaret Cavendish visits London, attending a meeting of the Royal Society, scandalizing Charles North with her extraordinary dress at a public playhouse, and attracting huge crowds behind her coach as she sojourns in Hyde Park. Publication of *The Life of William Cavendishe*. William Cavendish writes *The Humourous Lovers* for public performance, possibly with the aid of John Dryden, William Davenant, or Thomas Shadwell.

1668 Publication of *Playes Never Before Printed*. Reissuing of *Observations upon Experimental Philosophy, The Blazing World, Orations of Divers Sorts, Grounds of Natural Philosophy,* and *Poems or Several Fancies*.

1671 Reissuing of *The World's Olio* and *Nature's Pictures*.

1673 Death of Margaret Cavendish (December 15); burial in Westminster Abbey (January 7, 1674).

1674 William Cavendish rewrites *A Pleasante & Merye Humor off a Roge* as *The Triumphant Widow*, perhaps with the assistance of Thomas Shadwell.

1675 Reissuing of *Life of William Cavendishe*.

1676 Death of William Cavendish, burial beside Margaret in Westminster Abbey. Publication of *Letters and Poems in Honour of the Incomparable Princess Margaret, Duchess of Newcastle*, ed. William Cavendish.

A Note on the Text.

Both *Bell in Campo* and *The Sociable Companions* are taken from their original editions of 1662 and 1668 respectively, since Cavendish's plays were never issued in a second contemporary edition. I have checked the copies held at Harvard's Houghton Library against those at the Bodleian Library, the British Library, and the Huntington Library, and have found no press variants. The spelling has been silently modernized, with the exception of characters' names, while speech prefixes have been expanded. Cavendish's punctuation has been left intact; standardized punctuation did not exist in the seventeenth century, and though this might seem bewildering at first, the thoughts expressed in her occasionally enormous sentences are eminently clear. The visual tumble of ideas one upon another also gives a vivid impression of the Duchess's process of thought, which is valuable in and of itself while helping to move the action of the plays forward. Stage directions, including asides, and typography have been adjusted to conform to present practices; stage directions added by me appear in square brackets. In composing explanatory notes, I have relied primarily upon *The Oxford English Dictionary*. I am also enormously indebted to Greg Bennett for his invaluable help in transcribing text and clarifying several obscure references.

BELL IN CAMPO

THE DEDICATION

To those that do delight in scenes and wit,
I dedicate my book, for those I writ;
Next to my own delight, for I did take
Much pleasure and delight these plays to make;
For all the time my plays a-making were,
My brain the stage, my thoughts were acting there.

THE EPISTLE DEDICATORY

My Lord,

My resolution was that[1] when I had done writing, to have dedicated all my works in gross to your Lordship; and I did verily believe that this would have been my last work: but I find it will not, unless I die before I have writ my other intended piece. And as for this book of plays, I believe I should never have writ them, nor have had the capacity nor ingenuity to have writ plays, had not you read to me some plays which your Lordship had writ, and lay[2] by for a good time to be acted, wherein your wit did create a desire in my mind to write plays also, although my plays are very unlike those you have writ, for your Lordship's plays have as it were a natural life, and a quick spirit in them, whereas mine are like dull dead statues, which is the reason I send them forth to be printed, rather than keep them concealed in hopes to have them first acted; and this advantage I have, that is, I am out of the fear of having them hissed off from the stage, for they are not like to come thereon; but were they such as might deserve applause, yet if Envy did make a faction against them, they would have had a public condemnation; and though I am not such a coward, as to be afraid of the hissing serpents, or stinged tongues of Envy, yet it would have

---

1   that] crossed out in pencil in Houghton F1
2   lay] lie F1

made me a little melancholy to have my harmless and innocent plays go weeping from the stage, and whipped by malicious and hard-hearted censurers; but the truth is, I am careless, for so I have your applause I desire no more, for your Lordship's approvement[1] is a sufficient satisfaction to me

My Lord,

Your Lordship's honest wife, and faithful servant,

M.N.

---

1   approvement] approval

AN INTRODUCTION

Enter 3 Gentlemen.

1. GENTLEMAN.   Come Tom will you go to a play?
2. GENTLEMAN.   No.
1. GENTLEMAN.   Why?
2. GENTLEMAN.   Because there are[1] so many words, and so lit-
    tle wit, as the words tire me more than the wit delights me;
    and most commonly there is but one good part or
    humour, and all the rest are forced in for to underline[2] that
    part, or humour; likewise not above one or two good
    actors, the rest are as ill actors as the parts they act, besides,
    their best and principal part or humour is so tedious, that I
    hate at last what I liked at first, for many times a part is very
    good to the third act, but continued to the fifth is stark
    naught.
1. GENTLEMAN.   The truth is, that in some plays the poet[3]
    runs so long in one humour, as he runs himself out of
    breath.
3. GENTLEMAN.   Not only the poet but the humour he writes
    of seems to be as broken-winded.
1. GENTLEMAN.   I have heard of a broken-winded horse, but
    never heard of a broken-winded poet, nor of a broken-
    winded play before.
3. GENTLEMAN   I wonder why poets will bind themselves, so
    as to make every humour they write, or present, to run
    quite through their play.
2. GENTLEMAN.   Bind say you? They rather give themselves
    line and liberty, nay they are so far from binding, as for the
    most part they stretch the line of a humour into pieces.
3. GENTLEMAN.   Let me tell you, that if any man should write
    a play wherein he should present an humour in one act,
    and should not continue it to the end: although it must be
    stretched, as you say, to make it hold out, he would be con-

---

1   are] is F1
2   underline]enterline F1
3   poet] Poets F1

demned, and not only accounted an ill poet, but no poet, for it would be accounted as ill as wanting a rhyme in a copy of verses, or a word too short, or too much in a number, for which a poet is condemned, and for a word that is not spelled right, he is damned for ever.

1. GENTLEMAN.   Nay, he is only damned if he doth not write strictly to the orthography.

3. GENTLEMAN.   Scholars only damn writers and poets for orthography, but for the others, they are damned by the generality: that is, not only all readers, but all that are but hearers of the works.

1. GENTLEMAN.   The generality for the most part is not foolishly strict, or rigid as particulars are.

3. GENTLEMAN.   Yes faith, they are led by one bell-weather like a company of silly sheep.

1. GENTLEMAN.   Well, if I were to write a play, I would write the length of a humour according to the strength of the humour and breadth of my wit. Let them judge me and condemn as they would; for though some of the past, and present ages be erroneously or maliciously foolish in such cases; yet the future ages may be more wise, and better natur'd as to applaud what the others have condemned. But prithee Tom let us go.

2. GENTLEMEN   No, I will not go for the reasons before mentioned, which are,[1] they tire me with their empty words, dull speeches, long parts, tedious acts, ill actors; and the truth is, there's not enough variety in an old play to please me.

1. GENTLEMAN   There is variety of that which is bad, as you have divided it, but it seems you love youth and variety in plays, as you do in mistresses.

3. GENTLEMAN   Plays delight amorous men as much as a mistress doth.

1. GENTLEMAN   Nay, faith more, for a man and his mistress are soon out of breath in their discourse, and then they know not what to say, and when they are at a non-plus, they

---

1   are] is F1

would be glad to be quit of each other, yet are ashamed to part so soon, and are weary to stay with each other long, when a play entertains them with Love, and requires not their answers, nor forceth their brains, nor pumps their wits, for a play doth rather fill them than empty them.

2. GENTLEMAN. Faith most plays do[1] rather fill the spectators with wind, than with substance, with noise, than with news.

1. GENTLEMAN This play that I would have you go to, is a new play.

2. GENTLEMAN But is there news in the play, that is (is there new wit, fancies, or new scenes) and not taken out of old stories, or old plays newly translated.

1. GENTLEMAN I know not that, but this play was writ by a lady, who on my conscience hath neither language, nor learning, but what is native and natural.

2. GENTLEMAN A woman write a play! Out upon it, out upon it, for it cannot be good, besides, you say she is a lady, which is the likelier to make the play worse, a woman and a lady to write a Play; fie, fie.

3. GENTLEMAN Why may not a lady write a good play?

2. GENTLEMAN No, for a woman's wit is too weak and too conceited to write a play.

1. GENTLEMAN But if a woman hath wit, or can write a good play, what will you say then.

2. GENTLEMAN Why, I will say nobody will believe it, for if it be good, they will think she did not write it, or at least say she did not, besides, the very being a woman condemns it, were it never so excellent and rare, for men will not allow women to have wit, or women to have reason, for if we allow them wit, we shall lose our preeminence.[2]

1. GENTLEMAN If you will not go Tom, farewell; for I will go see this play, let it be good, or bad.

2. GENTLEMAN Nay stay, I will go with thee, for I am contented to cast away so much time for the sake of the sex. Although I have no faith of the authoress' wit.

---

1 do] doth F1
2 preeminence] prehemency F1

3. GENTLEMAN   Many a reprobate hath been converted and brought to repentance by hearing a good sermon, and who knows but that you may be converted from your erroneous opinion; by seeing this Play, and brought to confess that a lady may have wit.

[*Exeunt*]

BELL IN CAMPO

The Lord General
Seigneur Valeroso
Monsieur la Hardy
Monsieur Compagnion
Monsieur Comerade[2]
Monsieur la Gravity
Captain Ruffell[3]
Captain Whiffell[4], and several other gentlemen
Doctor Educature[5]
Doctor Comfort
Stewards, Messengers and Servants.
Lady Victoria
Madam Jantil[6]
Madam Passionate
Madam Ruffell
Madam Wiffell
Doll Pacify, Madam Passionate's maid
Nell Careless, Madam Jantil's maid
Other Servants and Heroickesses[7]

---

1 A similar dramatis personae list is given at the beginning of *The Second Part of Bell in Campo* in F1; I have chosen to omit the repetition here.

2 Comerade] A variant spelling of the modern "Comrade." Cavendish was fond of giving her characters suitably indicative names. I have retained the original spelling of all proper names.

3 Ruffell] A misspelling of "Ruffle."

4 Whiffell] Evidently a spelling variation on "Whistle."

5 Educature] A pun on "Education"; Cavendish was notoriously suspicious of higher education and often referred to her relative lack of formal education as a benefit to her writing.

6 Jantil] A near-phonetic spelling of the French *gentille*, meaning "gentle," "kind," "calm," or "tranquil."

7 Heroickesses] Cavendish used the term "heroickesses," rather than "heroines," to refer to female heroes, following her practice of feminizing male roles by adding "ess" (hence "Generaless," "Tutoress," and so on). Similarly, she calls male heroes "heroicks"; I have maintained both "heroick" and "heroickess" in particular throughout the text because of the emphasis the feminized term places on the extraordinary physical achievements of the women concerned.

THE FIRST PART OF BELL IN CAMPO

ACT I

SCENE 1

Enter two gentlemen.

1 GENT   You hear how this Kingdom of Reformation is preparing for war against the Kingdom of Faction.

2 GENT   Yea, for I hear the Kingdom of Faction resolves to war with this Kingdom of Reformation.

1 GENT.   'Tis true, for there are great preparations of either side, men are raised of all sorts and ages fit to bear arms, and of all degrees to command and obey, and there is one of the gallantest and noblest persons in this kingdom, who[1] is made General to command in chief; for he is a man that is both valiant and well experienced in wars, temperate and just in peace, wise and politic in public affairs, careful and prudent in his own family, and a most generous person.

2 GENT   Indeed I have heard that he is a most excellent soldier.

1 GENT   He is so, for he is not one that sets forth to the wars with great resolutions and hopes, and returns with masked[2] fears and despairs; neither is he like those that take more care, and are more industrious to get gay clothes, and fine feathers, to flaunt in the field, and vapour in their march, than to get useful and necessary provision; but before he will march, he will have all things ready and proper for use, as to fit himself with well-tempered arms, which are light to be worn, yet musket-proof; for he means not to run away, nor to yield his life upon easy terms unto his enemy; for he desires to conquer, and not vain-gloriously to show his courage by a careless neglect or a vain carelessness; also

---

1   who] which F1
2   masked] maskerd F1

he chooses such horses as are useful in war, such as have been made subject to the hand and heel, that have been taught to trot on the haunches, to change, to gallop, to stop, and such horses as have spirit and strength, yet quiet and sober natures; he regards more the goodness of the horses than the colours or marks, and more the fitness of his saddles than the embroidery; also he takes more care that his wagons should be easy to follow, and light in their carriage, than to have them painted and gilded; and he takes greater care that his tents should be made, so as to be suddenly put up, and as quickly pulled down, than for the setting and embroidering his arms thereupon; also he takes more care to have useful servants than numerous servants; and as he is industrious and careful for his particular affairs, so he is for the general affairs.

2 GENT. A good soldier makes good preparations, and a good general doth both for himself and army; and as the General hath showed himself a good soldier by the preparations he had made to march, so he hath shown himself a wise man by the settlement he hath made, in what he hath to leave behind him; for I hear he hath settled and ordered his house and family.

1 GENT He hath so, and he hath a fair young and virtuous lady that he must leave behind him, which cannot choose but trouble him.

2 GENT. The wisest man that is, cannot order or have all things to his own contentment.

Exeunt.

SCENE 2

Enter the Lord General, and the Lady Victoria his wife.

GENERAL My dear heart, you know I am commanded to the wars, and had I not such wife as you are, I should have thought Fortune had done me a favour to employ my life in heroic[1] actions for the service of my country, or to give me an honourable death, but to leave you is such a cross as my nature sinks under; but wheresoever you are there will be my life, I shall only carry a body which may fight, but my soul and all the powers thereof will remain with thee.

LADY VICTORIA Husband, I shall take this expression of love but for feigning words, if you leave me; for 'tis against Nature to part with that we love best, unless it be for the beloved's preservation, which cannot be mine, for my life lives in yours, and the comfort of that life in your company.

LORD GENERAL I know you love me so well, as you had rather part with my life than I should part from my honour.

LADY VICTORIA 'Tis true, my love persuades me so to do, knowing fame is a double life, as infamy is a double death; nay I should persuade you to those actions, were they never so dangerous, were you unwilling thereunto, or could they create a world of honour, fully inhabited with praises; but I would not willingly part with your life for an imaginary or supposed honour, which dies in the womb before it is born; thus I love you the best, preferring the best of what is yours; but I am but in the second place in your affections, for you prefer your honour before me; 'tis true, it is the better choice, but it shows I am not the best beloved, which makes you follow and glue to that and leave me.

LORD GENERAL Certainly wife my honour is your honour, and your honour will be buried in my disgrace, which Heaven avert; for I prefer yours before my own, insomuch as I would have your honour to be the crown of my glory.

LADY VICTORIA Then I must partake of your actions, and go along with you.

LORD GENERAL What to the wars?

LADY VICTORIA To any place where you are.

LORD GENERAL But wife you consider not, as that long marches, ill lodgings, much watching, cold nights, scorching days, hunger and danger are ill companions for ladies,

---

1 heroic] Heroical F1

their acquaintance displeases; their conversation is rough and rude, being too boisterous for ladies; their tender and strengthless constitutions cannot encounter nor grapple therewith.

LADY VICTORIA   'Tis said, that love overcomes all things: in your company long marches will be but as a breathing walk, the hard ground feel as a feather-bed, and the starry sky a spangled canopy, hot days a stove to cure cold agues, hunger as fasting days or an eve to devotion, and danger is honour's triumphant chariot.

LORD GENERAL   But Nature hath made women like china, or porcelain, they must be used gently, and kept warily, or they will break and fall on death's head: besides, the inconveniences in an army are so many, as put patience herself out of humour; besides, there is such inconveniences as modesty cannot allow of.

LADY VICTORIA   There is no immodesty in natural effect, but in unnatural abuses; but contrive it as well you can, for go I must, or either I shall die, or dishonour you; for if I stay behind you, the very imaginations of your danger will torture me, sad dreams will affright me, every little noise will sound as your passing bell, and my fearful mind will transform every object like as your pale ghost, until I am smothered in my sighs, shrouded in my tears, and buried in my griefs; for whatsoever is joined with true love, will die absented, or else their love will die, for love and life are joined together; as for the honour of constancy, or constant fidelity, or the dishonour of inconstancy, the lovingest and best wife in all story that is recorded to be, the most perfectest and constantest wife in her husband's absence was Penelope, Ulysses' wife,[1] yet she did not barricade[2] her ears from love's soft alarums; but parleyed and received

---

1   Penelope ... Ulysses] In Greek mythology, when Ulysses was absent from home for years during his voyages and adventures after the Trojan war, his wife Penelope remained unshakably faithful to him despite the importuning of many suitors. She told her suitors she would finally choose one of them once she had finished the weaving on her loom, and made sure to unpick each day's work at night.
2   barricade] Barricado F1

amorous treaties, and made a truce until she and her lovers could agree and conclude upon conditions, and question-less there were amorous glances shot from loving eyes of either party; and though the siege of her chastity held out, yet her husband's wealth and estate was impoverished, and great riots committed both in his family and kingdom, and her suitors had absolute power thereof; thus though she kept the fort of her chastity, she lost the kingdom, which was her husband's estate and government, which was a dis-honour both to her and to her husband; so if you let me stay behind you, it will be a thousand to one but either you will lose me in death, or your honour in life, where if you let me go you will save both; for if you will consider and reckon all the married women you have heard or read of, that were absented from their husbands, although upon just and necessary occasions, but had some ink of aspersions flung upon them, although their wives were old, ill-favoured, decrepit and diseased women, or were they as pure as light, or as innocent as Heaven; and wheresoever this ink of aspersion is thrown, it sticks so fast, that the spots are never rubbed out, should it fall on saints, they must wear the marks as a badge of misfortunes, and what man had not better be thought or called an uxorious husband, than to be despised and laughed at, as being but thought a cuckold? the first only expresses a tender and noble nature, the second sounds as a base, cowardly, poor, dejected, for-saken creature; and as for the immodesty you mentioned, there is none, for there can be no breach of modesty, but in unlawful actions, or at least unnecessary ones; but what law can warrant, and necessity doth enforce, is allowable amongst men, pure before angels, religious before gods, when un-choosing persons, improper places, unfit times, condemn those actions that are good in themselves, make them appear base to men, hateful to angels, and wicked to gods, and what is more lawful, fitting, and proper, than for a man and wife to be inseparable together?

LORD GENERAL   Well, you have used so much rhetoric to persuade, as you have left me none to deny you, wherefore I
am resolved you shall try what your tender sex can endure;
but I believe when you hear the bullets fly about you, you
will wish yourself at home, and repent your rash adventure.
LADY VICTORIA   I must prove false first, for love doth give me
courage.
LORD GENERAL   Then come along, I shall your courage try.
LADY VICTORIA   I'll follow you, though in Death's arms I lie.

[*Exeunt*]

SCENE 3

Enter the two former gentlemen

1 GENT   Well met, for I was going to thy lodging to call thee
to go make up the company of good fellows, which hath
appointed a meeting.
2 GENT   Faith you must go with the odd number, or get
another in my room, for I am going about some affairs
which the Lord General hath employed me in.
1 GENT   I perceive by thee that public employments spoil private meetings.
2 GENT   You say right, for if everyone had good employment,
vice would be out of fashion.
1 GENT   What do you call vice?
2 GENT   Drinking, wenching, and gaming.
1 GENT   As for two of them, as drinking and wenching, especially wenching, no employment can abolish them, no, not
the most severe, devote, nor dangerous: for the states-man
divines, and soldiers, which are the most and greatest
employed, will leave all other affairs to kiss a mistress.
2 GENT   But would you have me go to a tavern and not to a
mistress.

1 GENT.   Why, you may have a mistress in a tavern if you please.

2 GENT   Well, if my other affairs will give me any leisure, I will come to you.

Exeunt.

SCENE 4

Enter four or five other gentlemen.

1 GENT   The Lord General was accounted a discreet and wise man, but he shows but little wisdom in this action of carrying his wife along with him to the wars, to be a clog at his heels, a chain to his hands, an encumbrance in his march, obstruction in his way; for she will be always puling and sick, and whining, and crying, and tired, and froward, and if her dog should be left in any place, as being forgotten, all the whole army must make a halt whilst the dog is fetched, and trooper after trooper must be sent to bring intelligence of the dog's coming, but if there were such a misfortune that the dog could not be found, the whole army must be dispersed for the search of it, and if it should be lost, then there must seem to be more lamentation for it than if the enemy had given us an entire defeat, or else we shall have frowns instead of preferments.[1]

2 GENT   The truth is, I wonder the General will trouble himself with his wife, when it is the only time a married man hath to enjoy a mistress without jealousy, a spritely sound wench, that may go along without trouble, with bag and baggage, to wash his linen, and make his field bed, and attend to his call, when a wife requires more attendance than sentries to watch the enemy.

3 GENT   For my part I wonder as much that any man should

---

1   This episode recalls one of the adventures of Queen Henrietta Maria upon her temporary return from Holland in 1642: see Appendix D below for a contemporary account.

be so fond of his wife as to carry her with him; for I am only glad of the wars, because I have a good pretence to leave my wife behind me; besides an army is a quiet, solitary place, and yields a man a peaceable life compared to that at home: for what with the faction and mutiny amongst his servants, and the noise the women make, for their tongues like as an alarum beat up quarters in every corner of the house, that a man can take no rest; besides every day he hath a set battle with his wife, and from the army of her angry thoughts, she sends forth such vollies of words with her gunpowder anger, and the fire of her fury, as breaks all the ranks and files of content, and puts happiness to an utter rout, so as for my part I am forced to run away in discontent, although some husbands will stay, and fight for the victory.

4 GENT   Gentlemen, gentlemen, pray condemn not a man for taking his lawful delight, or for ordering his private affairs to his own humour, every man is free to himself, and to what is his, as long as he disturbs not his neighbours, nor breaks the peace of the kingdom, nor disorders the commonwealth, but submits to the laws, and obeys the magistrates without dispute; besides gentlemen, 'tis no crime nor wonder, for a man to let his wife go along with him when he goes to the wars, for there hath been examples; for Pompey had a wife with him, and so had Germanicus, and so had many great and worthy heroicks, and as for Alexander the great he had a wife or two with him;[1] besides, in many nations men are not only desired, but commanded by the chiefs to let their wives go with them, and it hath been a practice by long custom, for women to be spectators in their battles, to encourage their fights, and so give fire to their spirits; also to attend them in their sicknesses, to cleanse their wounds, to dress their meat; and who is fitter than a wife? what other woman will be so lovingly careful, and industriously helpful as a wife? and if the

---

1   Pompey, Germanicus, Alexander] All of these are famous classical generals (Pompey and Germanicus were Roman, Alexander Greek), known for their valour and unparalleled success in warfare.

Greeks had not left their wives behind them, but had carried them along to the Trojan wars, they would not have found such disorders as they did at their return, nor had such bad welcome home, as witness Agamemnon's; besides, there have been many women that have not only been spectators, but actors, leading armies, and directing battles with good success, and there have been so many of these heroicks, as it would be tedious at this time to recount; besides the examples of women's courage in death, as also their wise conduct, and valiant actions in wars are many, and pray give me leave to speak without your being offended thereat, it is not noble, nor the part of a gentleman, to censure, condemn, or dispraise another man's private actions, which nothing concerns him, especially when there is so gallant a subject to discourse of as the discipline and actions of these wars we are entering into.

I GENT   In truth, sir, you have instructed us so well, and have chided us so handsomely, as we are sorry for our error, and ask pardon for our fault, and our repentance shall be known by that we will never censure so again.

Exeunt.

ACT II

SCENE 5

Enter Captain Whiffell, and Madam Whiffell his wife.

CAPTAIN WHIFFELL I have heard our General's lady goeth with the General her husband to the wars, wherefore I think it fit for the rest of the commanders, if it were only for policy, to let our General see that we approve of his actions so well, as to imitate him in ours, carrying our wives along with us, besides the General's lady cannot choose but take it kindly to have our wives wait upon her, wherefore wife it is fit you should go.

MADAM WHIFFELL Alas husband I am so tender, that I am apt to catch cold if the least puff of wind do but blow upon me; wherefore to lie in the open fields will kill me the first night, if not, the very journey will shatter my small bones to pieces.

CAPTAIN WHIFFELL Why, our General's lady is a very fine young lady, and she ventures to go.

MADAM WHIFFELL There let her venture, for you must excuse me, for I will stay at home, go you where you please.

CAPTAIN WHIFFELL Well wife consider it.

Exeunt.

SCENE 6

Enter Captain Ruffell, and his wife Madam Ruffell.

CAPTAIN RUFFELL Wife prepare yourself to follow the army, for 'tis now the fashion for wives to march, wherefore pack up and away.

MADAM RUFFELL What with a knapsack behind me as your trull? Not I, for I will not disquiet my rest with inconveniences, nor divert my pleasures with troubles, nor be affrighted with the roaring cannons, nor endanger my life with every pot-gun, nor be frozen up with cold, nor stew'd to a jelly with heat, nor be powdered up with dust, until I come to be as dry as a neat's tongue; besides, I will not venture my complexion to the wrath of the sun, which will tan me like a sheep's skin.

CAPTAIN RUFFELL   Faith wife, if you will not go, I will have a laundry-maid to ride in my wagon, and lie in my tent.

MADAM RUFFELL   Prithee husband take thy kitchen maid along too, for she may have as much grease about her as will serve to make soap for your linen with, and while you ride with your laundry-maid in your wagon, I will ride with my gentleman-usher in my coach.

CAPTAIN RUFFELL   Why wife, it is out of love that I would have thee go.

MADAM RUFFELL   And 'tis out of love that I will stay at home; besides, do you think I mean to follow your General's lady as a common trooper doth a commander, to feed upon her reversions, to wait for her favour, to watch for a smile; no, no, I will be Generalissimo myself at home, and distribute my colours to be carried in the hats of those that will fight in my quarrel, to keep or gain the victory of my favour and love.

CAPTAIN RUFFELL   So I may chance to be a cuckold before I return home.

MADAM RUFFELL   You must trust to Fortune for that, and so I wish you a good journey.

Exeunt.

SCENE 7

*Enter Seigneur Valeroso and his friend Monsieur la Hardy, to take
their leaves of their wives, Madam Jantil, and Madam Passionate,
Madam Jantil young and beautiful,
Madam Passionate in years.*

MADAM JANTIL   I cannot choose but take it unkindly that
you will go without me; do you mistrust my affection? as
that I have not as much love for you as the General's lady
hath for her husband; or do you desire to leave me?
because you would take a mistress along with you, one that
perchance hath more beauty than you think me to have;
with whom you may securely and freely sit in your tent,
and gaze upon; or one that hath more wit than I, whose
sweet, smooth, and flattering words may charm your
thoughts, and draw your soul out of your ears to sit upon
her lips, or dancing with delight upon her tongue.

SEIGNEUR VALEROSO   Prithee wife be not jealous, I vow to
Heaven no other beauty can attract my eyes but thine, nor
any found can please my brain, but what thy charming
tongue sends in; besides, I prize not what thy body is, but
how thy soul's adorn'd, thy virtue would make me think
thee fair, although thou wert deformed, and wittier far
than Mercury, hadst thou Midas's ears, but thou hast all that
man can wish of womenkind, and that is the reason I will
leave thee safe at home; for I am loath to venture all my
wealth and happiness in Fortune's inconstant bark, suffer-
ing thy tender youth and sex to float on the rough waves of
chance, where dangers like to northern winds blow high,
and who can know but that fatal gusts may come, and
overwhelm thee, and drown all my joys? wherefore for my
sake keep thyself safe at home.

MADAM JANTIL   I shall obey you, but yet I think it were not
well I should be a long time from you, and at a great distance.

SEIGNEUR VALEROSO   I will promise you, if I perceive the
war is like to be prolonged, and that there be garrison

towns so safe as you may securely live in, I will send for you, placing you so where sometimes I may visit you.

MADAM JANTIL   Pray do not forget me so much as to cancel your promise.

SEIGNEUR VALEROSO   Forget thee, sweet? I should sooner forget life, and if I do whilst I have memory, Heaven forget me.

MADAM JANTIL   I must ask you a question, which is to know why you will take an under command, being so nobly born, and bearing a high title of Honour yourself, and being master of a great estate.

SEIGNEUR VALEROSO   To let the world see my courage is above my birth, wealth, or pride, and that I prefer inward worth before outward title, and I had rather give my life to the enemy on honourable terms, than basely to stay at home in time of general wars, out of an ambitious discontent: for valour had rather have dangers to fight with, than offices to command in.

Seigneur Valeroso and his lady whisper, while the other two Monsieur la Hardy and his lady speak.

MADAM PASSIONATE   Why should you go to the wars now you are in years, and not so fit for action as those that are young, and have their strengths about them? besides, we have lived a married pair above these thirty years, and never parted, and shall we now be separated when we are old?

She weeps.

MONSIEUR LA HARDY   Alas wife, what would you have me do? When I am commanded out I must obey; besides, I would not have my country fight a battle whilst I live, and I not make one, for all the world, for when I cannot fight, my body shall serve to stop a breach; wherefore leave your crying wife, and fall to praying for our safe return, and here my noble friend is desirous you should stay with his lady to comfort one another, and to divert melancholy and the longing hours of our return.

MADAM PASSIONATE Farewell, I fear I shall never see you again, for your absence will soon kill me.

She cries.

Exeunt.

SCENE 8

Enter two gentlemen.

1 GENT. O you are welcome from the army, what news?

2 GENT. Why our army march'd until they came unto the frontiers of the kingdom, where they found the army of the enemy ready to encounter them, the Lord General seeing they must of necessity fight a battle, thought best to call a council of war, that there might be nothing of ill conduct laid to his charge, but that all might be ordered by a wise and experienced council, whereupon he made an election of counselors, joining together three sorts,[1] as grave, wise, and prudent men, subtle and politic men, and valiant, skilful, martial men, that the cold temper of the prudent, might allay the hot temper of the valiant, and that the politic might be as ingenious[2] to serve them together by subtle devices, and to make traps of stratagems to catch in the enemy, and at this council many debates there were, but at last they did conclude a battle must be fought; but first they did decree that all the women should be sent into one of their garrison towns, some two days' journey from the army, the reasons were, that if they should be overcome by their enemies, the women might be taken by their enemies, and made slaves, using or abusing them as they

---

1 sorts] fots F1
2 ingenious] crossed out in pencil, with 'Enquie'? in margin, Houghton copy of F1

pleased; but when the women were sent away, they did not shed tears of sorrow, but sent such vollies of angry words, as wounded many men's hearts; but when they were almost at the town that was to be their abode, the General's lady, was too extremely incensed against the counselors, by reason they decreed her departure with the others, as she strove to raise up the spirits of the rest of her sex to the height of her own; but what the issue will be I know not.

1 GENT   Have you been with the King?

2 GENT   Yes, I was sent to give him an account of the army.

Exeunt.

SCENE 9

Enter the Lady Victoria and a number of women of all sorts with her, she takes her stand upon a heap of green turfs, as being in the fields before the garrison town, and then speaks to those women.

LADY VICTORIA   Most heroic spirits of most chaste and loving wives, mistresses, sisters, children or friends, I know you came not from your several houses and homes into this army merely to enjoy your husbands, lovers, parents and friends in their safe and secure garrisons, or only to share of their troublesome and tedious marches, but to venture also in their dangerous and cruel battles, to run their fortunes, and to force destiny to join you to their periods; but the masculine sex hath separated us, and cast us out of their companies, either out of their loving care and desire of preserving our lives and liberties, lest we might be destroyed in their confusions, or taken prisoners in their loss, or else it must be out of jealousy we should eclipse the fame of their valours with the splendor of our constancy; and if it be love, let us never give the preeminence, for then we should lose that prerogative that belongs to the crown of our sex; and if it be through jealous mistrust of their fame, it were poor for us to submit and quit that unto men, that men will not unto us, for fame makes us like the gods, to live for ever; besides, those women that have stayed at home will laugh at us in our return, and their effeminate lovers and carpet knights, that cowardly and luxuriously coin excuses to keep and stay them from the wars, will make lampoons of us for them to sing of our disgrace, saying, our husbands, lovers, and friends were so weary of us, as they were forced to take that pretence of affectionate love to be rid of our companies; wherefore if you will take my advice, let us return, and force those that sent us away to consent that we shall be partakers with them, and either win them by persuasions, or lose ourselves by breaking their decrees; for it were better we should die by their angry frown, than by the tongue of infamy.

All the women call to her.

ALL THE WOMEN   Let us return, let us return.

Lady Victoria waves her hand to them to keep silence.

LADY VICTORIA   Noble heroickesses, I am glad to hear you speak all as with one voice and tongue, which shows your minds are joined together, as in one piece, without seam or rent; but let us not return unfit to do them service, so we may cause their ruin by obstruction, which will wound us more than can their anger; wherefore let us strive by our industry to render ourselves useful to their service.
ALL THE WOMEN   Propound the way, and set the rules, and we will walk in the one, and keep strictly to the other.
LADY VICTORIA   Then thus, we have a body of about five or six thousand women, which came along with some thirty thousand men, but since we came, we are not only thought unuseful, but troublesome, which is the reason we were sent away, for the masculine sex is of an opinion we are only fit to breed and bring forth children, but otherwise a

trouble in a commonwealth, for though we increase the commonwealth by our breed, we encumber it by our weakness, as they think, as by our incapacities, as having no ingenuity for inventions, nor subtle wit for politicians; nor prudence for direction, nor industry for execution; nor patience for opportunity, nor judgement for counselors, nor secrecy for trust; nor method to keep peace, nor courage to make war, nor strength to defend our selves or country, or to assault an enemy; also that we have not the wisdom to govern a commonwealth, and that we are too partial to sit in the seat of justice, and too pitiful to execute rigorous authority when it is needful, and the reason for all of these erroneous opinions of the masculine sex to the effeminate, is, that our bodies seem weak, being delicate and beautiful, and our minds seem fearful, being compassionate and gentle natured, but if we were both weak and fearful, as they imagine us to be, yet custom which is a second nature will encourage the one and strengthen the other, and had our educations been answerable to theirs, we might have proved as good soldiers and privy counselors, rulers and commanders, navigators and architects, and as learned scholars both in arts and sciences, as men are; for time and custom are the father and mother of strength and knowledge, they make all things easy and facile, clear and propitious; they bring acquaintance, and make friendship of every thing; they make courage and fear, strength and weakness, difficulty and facility, dangers and securities, labours and recreations, life and death, all to take and shake as it were hands together; wherefore if we would but accustom ourselves we may do such actions, as may gain us such a reputation, as men might change their opinions, insomuch as to believe we are fit to be copartners in their governments, and to help to rule the world, where now we are kept as slaves forced to obey; wherefore let us make ourselves free, either by force, merit, or love, and in order, let us practice and endeavour, and take that which fortune shall proffer unto us, let us practice I say, and make these fields as schools of martial arts and sciences, so shall we become learned in their disciplines of war, and if you please to make me your tutoress, and so your generalless, I shall take the power and command from your election and authority, otherwise I shall most willingly, humbly, and obediently submit to those whom you shall choose.

ALL THE WOMEN You shall be our generalless, our instructress, ruler and commanderess, and we will everyone in particular, swear to obey all your commands, to submit and yield to your punishments, to strive and endeavour to merit your rewards.

LADY VICTORIA Then worthy heroickesses, give me leave to set the laws and rules I would have you keep and observe, in a brass tablet.

ALL THE WOMEN We agree and consent to whatsoever you please.

Exeunt.

SCENE 10

Enter the Lady Jantil alone.

MADAM JANTIL How painful is true love absented from what is loved, 'tis strange that which pleaseth most should be the greatest torment.

Enter Madam Passionate.

MADAM PASSIONATE What, all times walking by yourself alone? when your lord returns I will complain, and tell him what dull company you are.

MADAM JANTIL I hope I shall not be from him so long, for he promised to send for me.

MADAM PASSIONATE Nay faith, when you go, as old as I am, I will travel with you to see my husband too.

MADAM JANTIL You will be so much the more welcome, by how much you were unexpected.

MADAM PASSIONATE You look pale on the sudden, are not you well?

MADAM JANTIL Yes, only on a sudden I had a chill of cold that seized on my spirits.

MADAM PASSIONATE Beshrew me, their coldness hath nipped the blood out of your cheeks and lips.

MADAM JANTIL If they had been painted, they would have kept their colour.

Exeunt.

ACT III

SCENE 11

Enter the Lady Victoria with a great company of women, after a table of brass carried before her, she stands upon the heap of turfs, and another woman that carried the table, wherein the laws and rules are inscribed; she bids her read them.

READER   Noble heroicks, these are the laws our Generalless hath caused to be inscribed[1] and read for every one to observe and keep. First, be it known, observed, and practiced, that no woman that is able to bear arms, shall go unarmed, having arms to wear, but shall wear them at all times, but when they put them off to change their linen; they shall sleep, eat and rest, and march with them on their bodies.

LADY VICTORIA   Give me leave noble heroicks to declare the reason of this law or command, as to wear an iron or steel habit, and to be so constantly worn, is, that your arms should not feel heavy, or be troublesome or painful for want of use, as they will be when you shall have an occasion to put them on; and certainly, for want of practice, more masculine soldiers are overcome by their arms, than by their enemies, for the unaccustomed-ness makes them so unwieldy, as they can neither defend themselves, nor assault their foes, whereas custom will make them feel as light, as their skins on their flesh, or their flesh on their bones, nay custom hath that force, as they will feel as if their bodies were naked, when as their arms are off, and as custom makes the cold and piercing air to have no power over the naked bodies of men, for in cold countries as well as hot, men have been accustomed to go naked, and have felt no more harm, nor so much, by the cold, than those that are warmly clothed, so custom will make your arms seem as light as if you had none on, when for want of use

---

1   inscribed] instribed F1

their weight will seem heavy, their several pieces trouble-some and cumbersome, as their gorgets[1] will seem to press down their shoulders, their back and breast-plates and the rest of the several pieces to cut their waists, to pinch their body, to bind their thighs, to tie their arms, and their head-piece to hinder their breath, to darken their sight, and to stop their hearing, and all for want of use and custom; but enough of this, read on.

READER   Secondly, be it known, observed and practiced, that every company must watch by turns, whether they have enemies near or no, and at all times, and whosoever drinks any thing but water, or eats any thing but bread, all the time they are on the watch shall be punished with fasting.

LADY VICTORIA   Give me leave to declare the reason of this law, the reason is, that strong drinks, and nourishing meats sent many vapours to the brain, which vapours are like several keys, which lock up the senses so fast, as neither loud noises, bright lights, nor strong scents can enter either at the ears, eyes, or nostrils, insomuch as many times their enemies send Death to break them asunder.

READER   Thirdly, be it known, observed and practiced, that none of the troopers march over corn fields if it can be avoided, unless the enemy should be behind, and then the more spoil the better.

LADY VICTORIA   The reason of this is, that it were a great imprudence to destroy through a careless march of horse and foot, that which would serve to feed and nourish us in the winter time, and in our winter quarters, when it is laid in the barns and granaries, by the labour and the industry of the farmers.

READER   Fourthly, be it known, observed and practiced, that none shall plunder those things which are weighty of car-riage, unless it be for safety or necessity.

LADY VICTORIA   The reason is of this, that all that is heavy in the carriage is a hindrance in our march.

---

1   gorgets] A gorget was a piece of armour that covered the throat; ironically, the term was also used to designate either a lady's wimple (that covered her head, neck, and breast) or a woman's necklace during the seventeenth century.

READER   Fifthly, be it known, observed, and practiced, that no soldiers shall play at any game for money or drink, but only for meat to eat.

LADY VICTORIA   The reason of this is, that those that play for drink, the winners will be drunk, and those that are drunk are unfit for service; besides, many disorders are caused by drunkenness; and to play for money, the losers grow choleric, and quarrels proceed therefrom, which quarrels many times cause great mutinies through their side taking, and factious parties, besides, having lost their money and not their appetites, they become weak and faint for want of that nourishing food, their money should get them, having nothing left to buy them victuals withal; besides, it forces them to forage further about, where by straggling far from the body of the army, they are subject to be catch'd by the enemy, but when they play for meat their winnings nourish their bodies, making them strong and vigorous, and when their appetites are satisfied, and their stomachs are fill'd, their humours are pleasant, and their minds courageous; besides, it is the nature of most creatures, either to distribute or at least to leave the remaining pieces to the next takers, so that the losers may have a share with the winners, and part of what was their own again.

READER   Sixthly, be it known, observed, and practiced, that no Captains or Colonels, shall advance beyond their company, troop, regiment or brigade, but keep in the middle of the first rank, and the Lieutenant, or Lieutenant Colonel to come behind in the last rank.

LADY VICTORIA   The reason of this is, that Colonels and Captains going a space before their troops, companies, or regiments, for to encourage and lead on their soldiers, do ill to set themselves as marks for the enemy to shoot at, and if the chief commanders should be kill'd, the common soldiers would have but faint hearts to fight, but for the most part they will run away, as being afraid and ashamed to see the enemy, when their chief commander is kill'd, and if they have no officer or commander behind them, the common soldiers will be apt to run away, having no worthy witnesses or judges, to view and condemn their base cowardly actions, which otherwise they are ashamed of, choosing rather to fight their enemies than to make known their fears.

READER   Seventhly, be it known, observed and practiced, that none of the army lie in garrison towns, but be always entrenched abroad.

LADY VICTORIA   The reason of this is, that towns breed or beget a tenderness of bodies and laziness of limbs, luxurious appetites, and soften the natural dispositions, which tenderness, luxury, effeminacy, and laziness, corrupts and spoils martial discipline, whereas the open fields, and casting up trenches makes soldiers more hardy, laborious and careful, as being more watchful.

READER[1]   Eighthly, be it known, observed and practiced, that none unless visibly sick to be idle, but employed in some masculine action, as when not employed against an enemy, and that they are not employed about the works, forts or trenches, but have spare time to employ themselves, in throwing the bar, tripping,[2] wrestling, running, vaulting, riding, and the like exercise. Ninthly, be it known, observed and practiced, that every commander when free from the enemy's surprises, shall train their men thrice a week at least, nay every day if they can spare so much time, as putting their soldiers into several ranks, files and figures, in several bodies apart, changing into several places, and the like.

LADY VICTORIA   The reason of this is, that the soldiers may be expert and ready, and not be ignorant when they encounter their enemies, for many a battle is lost more through the ignorance of the soldiers, not being well and carefully train'd by their commanders, or having such commanders that know not how to train or draw them up, there are more battles I say lost thus, than for want of men or courage.

---

1   *Reader*] no change of speaker noted with change of line in F1; the rules beginning with "Ninthly" are preceded by a speech prefix, which I have omitted for clarity.

2   Tripping] crossed out in pencil with "Pitching" written in margin in Houghton copy of F1.

READER   Tenthly, be it known, observed and practiced, that every morning when encamped, that every commander shall make and offer in the midst of his soldiers a prayer to Mars, another to Pallas,[1] a third to Fortune, and a fourth to Fame; these prayers to be presented to these gods and goddesses with great ceremony, both from the commander and common soldiers.

LADY VICTORIA   The reason of this is, that ceremony strikes a reverence and respect into every breast, raising up a devotion in every heart, and devotion makes obedience, and obedience keeps order, and order is the strength and life to an army, state, or commonwealth; and as for the prayers presented to these particular gods and goddesses, [the reason] is, that Mars would give us courage and strength, Pallas give us prudent conduct, Fortune give us victory, and Fame give us glory and renown.

READER   Eleventhly, be it known, observed and practiced, that the most experienced, practiced, and ingenious commanders shall preach twice a week of martial discipline, also those errors that have been committed in former wars, and what advantages have been taken, to be cited in their sermons, as also what was gain'd or lost by mere fortune. Twelfthly, be it known, observed and practiced, that when the army marches, that the soldiers shall sing in their march the heroic actions done in former times by heroic women.

LADY VICTORIA   The reason of this is, that the remembrance of the actions of gallant persons inflames the spirit to the like, and begets a courage to a like action, and the reason of singing of heroic actions only of women, is that we are women ourselves.

READER   Thirteenthly, be it known, observed and submitted to, that no council shall be call'd, but that all affairs be ordered and judged by the Generalless herself.

LADY VICTORIA   The reason of this is, that all great councils, as of many persons, confound judgements, for most being of several opinions, and holding strongly and stiffly, nay

---

1   Pallas] An alternate name for Athena, the Greek goddess of wisdom and warfare (including battle strategy and tactics).

obstinately thereunto, as everyone thinking themselves wisest, cause a division, and wheresoever a division is there can be no final conclusion.

READER   Fourteenthly, be it known, observed and practiced, that none of this effeminate army admits of the company of men, whilst they are in arms or warlike actions, not so much as to exchange words, without the Generalless her leave or privilege thereto.

LADY VICTORIA   The reason of this is, that men are apt to corrupt the noble minds of women, and to alter their gallant, worthy, and wise resolutions, with their flattering words, and pleasing and subtle insinuations, and if they have any authority over them, as husbands, fathers, brothers, or the like, they are apt to fright them with threats into a slavish obedience; yet there shall be chosen some of the most inferior of this female army, to go into the masculine army, to learn their designs, and give us intelligence of their removals, that we may order our encampings and removings according as we shall think best; but these women shall neither be of the body of our army, nor keep amongst the army, nor come within the trenches, but lie without the works in huts, which shall be set up for that purpose.

READER   Lastly, whosoever shall break any of these laws or orders, shall be put to death, and those that do not keep them strictly, shall be severely punished.

LADY VICTORIA   But I am to advise you noble heroicks, that though I would not have a general council call'd to trouble our designs in war with tedious disputes, and unnecessary objections, and over cautious doubts, yet in case of life and death, there shall be a jury chosen to sit and judge their causes, and the whole army shall give their votes, and the most voices shall either condemn, or reprieve, or save them, lest I should hereafter be only call'd in question, and not the rest, as being not accessory thereunto; and now you have heard these laws or orders, you may assent or dissent therefrom as you please, if you assent, declare it by setting your hands thereto, if you dissent, declare it by word of mouth, and the tables shall be broken.

ALL THE WOMEN   We assent, and will set our hands thereto.

Exeunt.

SCENE 12

*Enter Doctor Educature the Lady Jantil's chaplain,
and Nell Careless her maid.*

DOCTOR EDUCATURE   Nell, how doth your good lady?

NELL CARELESS   Faith she seems neither sick nor well, for
though her body seems in health, her mind seems to be full
of trouble, for she will rise in the midst of the night, and
walk about her chamber only with her mantle about her.

DOCTOR EDUCATURE   Why doth she so?

NELL CARELESS   I ask'd her why she broke her sleep so as to
walk about, and she answered me, that it was frightful
dreams that broke her sleep, and would not let her rest in
quiet.

DOCTOR EDUCATURE   Alas she is melancholic in the absence
of my lord.

Exeunt.

SCENE 13

Enter the Lady Victoria and a number of other women.

LADY VICTORIA   Now we are resolved to put ourselves into a
warlike body, our greatest difficulty will be to get arms; but
if you will take my advice we may be furnished with those
necessaries, as thus, the garrison we are to enter is full of
arms and ammunition, and few men to guard them, for not
only most of the soldiers are drawn out to strengthen the
General's army, and to fight in the battle but as many of the
townsmen as are fit to bear arms; wherefore it must of

necessity be very slenderly guarded, and when we are in the town, we will all agree in one night, when they shall think themselves most secure, to rise and surprise those few men that are left, and not only disarm them and possess ourselves of the town and all the arms and ammunition, but we will put those men out of the town or in safe places, until such time as we can carry away whatsoever is useful or needful for us, and then to go forth and entrench, until such time as we have made ourselves ready to march, and being once master or mistress of the field we shall easily master the peasants, who are for the most part naked and defenceless, having not arms to guard them, by which means we may plunder all their horses, and victual ourselves out of their granaries; besides, I make no question but that our army will increase numerously by those women that will adhere to our party, either out of private and home discontents, or for honour and fame, or for the love of change, and as it were a new course of life; wherefore let us march to the town and also to our design, but first I must have you all swear secrecy.

ALL THE WOMEN   We are all ready to swear to what you will have us.

Exeunt.

SCENE 14

Enter Madam Jantil alone as rising out of her bed, her mantle wrapt about her, and in her night linen.

MADAM JANTIL   I saw his face pale as a lily white,[1]

---

1   This scene marks the first use of verse in this play. While the vast majority of the text is written in prose, Cavendish seems to have preferred to use the heightened language of verse for the scenes involving Jantil's reminiscing and mourning for her husband, as a way of furthering the poignancy of these scenes, perhaps. It is also notable that the Marquis of Newcastle's contributions to the play (in the form of songs) are also all in verse: in adding to his wife's work, he clearly preferred to do so through a particularly artistic medium.

His wounds fresh bleeding blood like rubies bright;
His eyes were looking steadfastly on me,
Smiling as joying in my company;
He mov'd his lips as willing was to speak,
But had no voice, and all his spirits weak;
He shak'd his hand as if he bid farewell,
That brought the message which his tongue would tell;
He's dead, he's dead, asunder break my heart,
Let's meet in death, though wars our lives did part.

After she had walkt silently a turn or two about her chamber her eyes
being fixt on the ground, she return'd as to her Bed.

Exit.

SCENE 15

Enter a Gentleman, and another meets him as in great haste.

1 GENT   What news? what news?
2 GENT   Sad news, for there hath been a battle fought betwixt
the two armies, and our army is beaten, and many of our
gallant men slain.
1 GENT.   I am sorry for that.

The second Gentleman goeth out.

Enter a third Gentleman.

1 GENT   Sir I suppose you are come newly from the army,
pray report the battle?
3 GENT   Truly I came not now from the army, but from the
town the General's heroic lady and the rest of the heroicks
did surprise, sieze and plunder.
1 GENT.   What the garrison town they were sent to for safety?
3 GENT   Yes.
1 GENT   And doth their number increase?

3 GENT   O very much, for after the surprising[1] of the town
the women in that town did so approve of their gallant
actions, as every one desired to be enlisted in the roll, and
number of the Amazonian[2] army, but in the mean time of
the forming of their army, intelligence was brought of the
battle which was fought, and that there was such loss of
both sides as each army retir'd back, being both so weak as
neither was able to keep the field, but that the loss was
greater on the reformed army, by reason there were so
many of their gallant men slain, but this news made many a
sad heart and weeping eyes in the female army; for some
have lost their husbands, some their fathers, others their
brothers, lovers and friends.

1 GENT   Certainly this will fright them out of the field of war,
and cause them to lay by their heroic designs.

3 GENT   I know not what they will do, for they are very secret
to their designs, which is strange, being all women.

Exeunt.

---

1   surprising] surprisal F1
2   Amazonian] The Amazons were a mythical race of warrior women, for whom men
served as domestic servants and procreators only.

ACT IV

SCENE 16

Enter two women like Amazons.

1 WOMAN   Our Generalless seems to be troubled, perceiving how heavily this female army takes their losses.

2 WOMAN   She hath reason, for it may hinder or at least obstruct her high designs.

Exeunt.

SCENE 17

*Enter the Lady Victoria and her Amazons,
she takes her stand and speaks to them.*

LADY VICTORIA   Noble heroicks, I perceive a mourning veil over the face of this female army, and it becomes it well; for 'tis both natural and human to grieve for the death of our friends; but consider constant heroicks, tears nor lamentations cannot call them out of the grave, no petitions can persuade Death to restore them, nor threats to let them go, and since you cannot have them alive being dead, study and be industrious to revenge their quarrels on their enemies' lives, let your justice give them death for death, offer upon the tombs of your friends the lives of their foes, and instead of weeping eyes, let us make them weep through their veins; wherefore take courage, cast off your black veil of sorrow, and take up the firematch of rage, that you may shoot revenge into the hearts of their enemies, to which I hope Fortune will favour us; for I hear that as soon as the masculine army have recovered strength there will be another battle fought, which may be a means to prove our loves to our friends, our hate to our enemies, and an aspiring to our honour and renown; wherefore let us employ our care to fit ourselves for our march.

ALL THE WOMEN We shall follow and obey you, where, and when, and how you please.

Exeunt.

SCENE 18

*Enter Doctor Educature and Nell Careless;
the Doctor weeps.*

DOCTOR EDUCATURE Doth my lady hear of my lord's death?

NELL CARELESS The messenger or intelligencer of my lord's death is now with her.

Exeunt.

SCENE 19

*Enter Madam Jantil, and a Gentleman Intelligencer;
the lady seems not disturb'd; but appears as usually.*

MADAM JANTIL How died my lord?

GENTLEMAN Madam, he fought with so much courage, as his actions will never die, and his valour will keep alive the memory of this war: for though he died, his death was crown'd with victory, he digg'd his grave out of his enemies' sides, and built his pyramid with heaps of their bodies; the groans of those he slew did ring his dying knell.

MADAM JANTIL What became of his body?

GENTLEMAN He gave order before the armies joined to fight, that if he were kill'd, his body should be sought out, and delivered to you: for he said it was yours whilst he lived, and he desired it might be disposed of by you when he was dead; his desires and commands were obeyed, and his body is coming in a litter lapped in serecloth.

MADAM JANTIL   Worthy sir, I give you many thanks for your
noble relation, assuring myself it is true because you report
it, and it is my husband that is the subject and ground of
that honourable relation, whom I always did believe would
out-act all words.

GENTLEMAN   He hath so madam.

MADAM JANTIL   Sir, if I can at any time honourably serve
you, I shall be ready whensoever you will command me.

GENTLEMAN   Your servant madam.

(He was going forth and returns)

If your Ladyship hath not heard of Monsieur la Hardy's
death, give me leave to tell you he is slain.

MADAM JANTIL   I am sorry, and for his lady, for she loved him
most passionately.[1]

The Gentleman goes out.

Enter as running and calling out Doll Pacify,
Madam Passionate's maid.

DOLL PACIFY   Help, help, my lady is dead, my lady is fallen
into a swoon at the report of my master's being kill'd.

The lady goeth out and the maid, then they enter straight again with
two or three servants more, bringing in the Lady Passionate
as in a swoon.

MADAM JANTIL   Alas poor lady, her spirits are drown'd in sorrow, and grief hath stopt her breath; loosen her garments,
for she is swell'd with troubled thoughts, her passions lie on
heaps, and so oppress life, it cannot stir, but makes her
senseless.

Upon the loosing of her garments she revives, and cries out.

---

1   passionately] passionably F1

MADAM PASSIONATE   O my husband, my husband!

She swoons again.

MADAM JANTIL   Bow her forward, bow her forward.

Madam Passionate revives again.

MADAM PASSIONATE   O let me die, let me die, and bury, bury me with him.

Swoons again.

MADAM JANTIL   Alas poor lady, put her to bed, for her life will find most ease there.

The Servants go out with Madam Passionate.

Madam Jantil alone.

MADAM JANTIL   O life what are thou? and Death where dost thou lead us, or what dissolv'st thou us into?

Exit.[1]

SCENE 20

Enter two Gentlemen.

1 GENT   I wonder there is no news or messenger come from the army yet, when there usually comes one every day.

Enter a Messenger.

2 GENT   O sir, what news?
MESSENGER   Faith there hath been nothing acted since the last

---

1   Exit] Exeunt F1

battle, but it is said there will be another battle very suddenly, for the enemy provokes our men to fight, by reason our Lord General lies sick of his wounds, having had a fever, caused by the anguish of his hurts, and by his sickness the enemies hope to gain an advantage of his absence, but he hath put a deputy in his place to command in chief until he recovers.

1 GENT   What is become of the female army?

MESSENGER   I hear they are marched towards the masculine army, but upon what design I cannot understand.

Exeunt.

SCENE 21

Enter Madam Jantil, and her maid Nell Careless.

MADAM JANTIL   Call my steward.

The maid goes out.

The lady walks in a musing posture, her eyes fixt on the ground.

Enter the steward weeping.

STEWARD   O madam, that I should live to hear this cursed news of my dear lord and master's death.

MADAM JANTIL   Life is a curse, and there's none happy but those that die in the womb before their birth, because they have the least share of misery; and since you cannot weep out life, bear it with patience; but thy tears have almost washed out the memory of what I was to say, but this it is, that I would have you sell all my jewels, plate, and household furniture to the best advantage, and to turn off all my servants, but just those to attend my person, but to reward all of them with something more than their wages, and those servants that are old, and have spent their youth with my lord's predecessors and in his service, but especially those he favoured most, give them so much during their lives as may keep them from the miseries of necessity, and vexations of poverty. Thirdly, I would have you hire the best and most curious[1] carvers or cutters of stones to make a tomb after my direction; as first I will have a marble piece raised from the ground about half a man's height or something more, and something longer than my husband's dead body, and then my husband's image carved out of marble to be laid thereupon, his image to be carved with his armor on, and half a head-piece on the head, that the face might be seen, which face I would have to the life as much as art can make it; also let there be two statues, one for Mercury,[2] and another for Pallas, these two statues to stand at his head, and the hands of these statues to join and to be laid under as carrying the head of my husband's figure, or as the head lay thereupon, and their hands as his pillow; on the right side of his figure, let there be a statue for Mars, and the hand of Mars's statue holding the right hand of my husband's figure, and on the left hand a statue for Hymen,[3] the hand on the place of the heart of my husband's figure, and at the feet of the figure let there be placed a statue for Fortune also, about a yard distance from the tomb; at the four corners thereof, let there be four marble pillars raised of an indifferent height, and an arched marble cover thereupon, and let all the ground be paved underneath with marble, and in the midst on the outside of the marble roof let the statue of Fame be placed in a flying posture, and as blowing a trumpet; then some two yards distance square from those pillars, let the ground be paved also with marble, and at the four corners four other marble pillars raised as high as the former, with capitals at top, and the body of those pillars round, and the statues of the four Cardinal

---

1   most curious] curioust F1
2   Mercury] The messenger of the gods in Roman mythology; he was also the god of roads, heralds (which would explain his presence here) and illicit dealings.
3   Hymen] The Greek god of matrimony.

Virtues placed on those capitals, sitting as in a weeping posture, and at the feet of those pillars the statues of the Graces embracing each pillar; as the statue of Charity, the pillar whereon the statue of Justice sits, and the statue of Patience, the pillar of Temperance, and the statue of Hope, the pillar of Prudence, and the statue of Faith, the pillar of Fortitude; then set a grove of trees all about the outside of them, as laurel, myrtle, cypress, and olive, for in death is peace, in which trees the birds may sit and sing his elegy; this tomb placed in the midst of a piece of ground of some ten or twenty acres, which I would have encompassed about with a wall of brick of a reasonable height, on the inside of the wall at one end, I would have built a little house divided into three rooms, as a gallery, a bed-chamber, and a closet, on the outside of the wall a house for some necessary servants to live in, to dress my meat, and to be ready at my call, which will be but seldom, and that by the ring of a bell, but the three rooms I would have furnished after this manner, my chamber and the bed therein to be hung with white, to signify the purity of chastity, wherein is no colours made by false lights; the gallery with several colours intermixed, to signify the varieties, changes, and encumbrances of life; my closet to be hung with black, to signify the darkness of death, wherein all things are forgotten and buried in oblivion; thus will I live a signification, not as a real substance but as a shadow made betwixt life and death; from this house which shall be my living tomb, to the tomb of my dead husband, I would have a cloister made, through which I may walk freely to my husband's tomb, from the injuries of the weather, and this cloister I would have all the sides thereof hung with my husband's pictures drawn to the life by the best painters, and all the several accidents, studies and exercise of his life; thus will I have the story of his life drawn to the life: see this my desire speedily, carefully, and punctually done, and I shall reward your service as a careful and diligent steward and servant.

STEWARD   It shall be done, but why will not your Ladyship have my lord's figure cast in brass?

MADAM JANTIL   Because the wars ruin tombs before Time doth, and metals being useful therein are often taken away by necessity, and we seldom find any ancient monuments but what are made of stone, for covetousness is apt to rob monuments of metal, committing sacrileges on the dead, for metals are soonest melted into profit, but stone is dull and heavy, creeping slowly, bringing but a cold advantage, wherein lies more pains than gains.

STEWARD   But your Ladyship may do all this without selling your jewels, plate, and household furniture.

MADAM JANTIL   It is true, but I would not let so much wealth lie dead in vanity, when exchanging them for money, I can employ it to some good use.

STEWARD   Your Ladyship hath forgotten to give order for blacks.

MADAM JANTIL   No I have not, but I will give no mourning until my husband's body be carried to the tomb; wherefore I have nothing more to employ you in at this time, but only to send hither my chaplain Doctor Educature.

The Steward goes out.

Enter Doctor Educature.

MADAM JANTIL   Doctor, although it is not the profession of a divine to be an historian, yet you knowing my husband's life and natural disposition best, being in his childhood under your tutorage, and one of his family ever since, I know none so proper for that work as you; and though you are naturally an eloquent orator, yet the bare truth of his worthy virtues and heroic actions will be sufficient to make the story both profitable, delightful, and famous; also I must entreat you to choose out a poet, one that doth not merely write for gain, or to express his own wit, so much as to endeavour to pencil with the pen virtue to the life, which in my lord was so beautiful as it was beyond all draughts, but the theme will inspire his muse, and when both these works are writ, printed and set out, as divulged to the world as a pattern for examples, which few will be able to imitate, then I would have these books lie by me as registers of memory, for next unto the gods my life shall be spent in contemplation of him; I know I shall not need to persuade you to do this, for your affection to his memory is ready of itself; but love and duty binds me to express my desires for his fame leaving nothing which is for my part thereunto.

DOCTOR EDUCATURE   Madam, all the service I can do towards the memory of my dear pupil, and noble lord and patron, shall be most devoutly observed and followed; for Heaven knows, if I had as many lives to dispose of as I have lived years, I would have sacrificed them all for to have redeemed his life from death.

Doctor Educature goes out.

Madam Jantil alone.

MADAM JANTIL   When I have interred my husband's body, and all my desires thereunto be finished, I shall be at some rest, and like an executrix to myself executing my own will, distributing the rites and ceremonies, as legacies to the dead, thus the living gives the dead; but O my spirits are tired with the heavy burden of melancholy, and grow faint for want of rest, yet my senses invite me thereunto, yet I cannot rest in my bed, for frightful dreams disturb me; wherefore I will lie down on this floor, and try if I can get a quiet sleep on the ground, for from earth I came, and to earth I would willingly return.

She lays herself down upon the ground, on one side of her arm bowing, leaning upon her elbow, her forehead upon the palm of her hand bowing forwards, her face towards the ground; but her grief elevating her passion, thus speaks

MADAM JANTIL   Weep cold earth, through your pores weep,
Or in your bowels my salt tears fast keep;

Inurn my sighs which from my grief is sent,
With my hard groans build up a monument;
My tongue like as a pen shall write his name,
My words as letters to divulge his fame;
My life like to an arch over his ashes bend,
And my desires to his grave descend;
I warn thee life keep me not company,
I am a friend to Death thy enemy;
For thou art cruel, and every thing torments,
Wounding with pain all that the world presents;
But Death is generous and sets us free,
Breaks off our chains, and gives us liberty;
Heals up our wounds of trouble with sweet rest,
Draws our corrupted passions from our breast;
Lays us to sleep on pillows of soft ease,
Rocks us with silence nothing hears nor sees.

She fetches a great sigh.

O that I may here sleep my last.

After a short slumber she wakes.

If it were not for dreams sleep would be a happiness next unto death; but I find I cannot sleep a long sleep in death, I shall not die so soon as I would.

Love is so strong and pure it cannot die,
Lives not in sense, but in the soul doth lie;
Why do I mourn? his love with mine doth dwell,
His love is pleas'd mine entertains it well;
But mine would be like his one embodied,
Only an essence or like a godhead

Exit.[1]

---

1   Exit] Exeunt F1

SCENE 22

Enter Doctor Comfort, and Doll Pacify.

DOCTOR COMFORT   How doth our lady Doll?

DOLL PACIFY   Today she began to sit up, but yet she is very weak and faint.

DOCTOR COMFORT   Heaven help her.

DOLL PACIFY   You that are Heaven's almoner, should distribute Heaven's gifts out of the purse of your mouth, and give her single godly words instead of single silver pence, to buy her some heavenly food to feed her famished mind.

DOCTOR COMFORT   Thou art a full-fed wench.

DOLL PACIFY   If I were no better fed than you feed me, which is but once a week, as on Sundays, I should be starved.

DOCTOR COMFORT   You must fast and pray, fast and pray.

Exeunt.

ACT V

SCENE 23

Enter two Gentlemen.

1 GENT. All the young gallants in the town are preparing themselves with fine clothes and feathers to go a-wooing to the two rich widows, the Lady Jantil, and the Lady Passionate

2 GENT Riches are the lodestone of affection, or at least professions.

1 GENT The truth is, riches draw more suitors, than youth, beauty, or virtue.

Exeunt.

SCENE 24

Enter two or three Gentlemen, Monsieur Comerade,
Monsieur Compagnion, and Monsieur la Gravity.

MONSIEUR COMERADE For Heaven's sake let us go and address ourselves to the two rich widows.

MONSIEUR COMPAGNION For my part I will address myself to none but the young widow, the Lady Jantil, and to her let us go without delay.

MONSIEUR LA GRAVITY It will be uncivil to go so soon after their husbands' deaths, for their husbands are not yet laid in their graves.

MONSIEUR COMPAGNION If they were we should come too late, for I knew a man which was a great friend of mine, who was resolved to settle himself in a married course of life, and so he went a-wooing to a widow, for a widow he was resolved to marry, and we went a-wooing to one whose husband was but just cold in his grave, but she told him she was promised before, so he wooed another whilst she followed her husband's corpse, but she told him he came too late, whereat he thought with the third not to be a second in his suit, and so expressed his desires in her husband's sickness, she told him she was very sorry that she had passed her word before to another, for if she had not, she would have made him her choice, whereat he cursed his imprudence, and wooed the fourth on her wedding day, who gave him a promise after her husband was dead to marry him, and withal she told him, that if she had been married before, it had been ten to one but he had spoke too late, for said she, when we are maids we are kept from the free conversation of men, by our parents or guardians, but on our wedding day we are made free and set at liberty, and like as young heirs on the day of one-and-twenty we make promises like bonds for two or three lives: wherefore I fear we shall miss our hopes, for these two widows will be promised before we address our suit.

MONSIEUR LA GRAVITY   No, for I am confident all do not so, for some love to have the freedoms of their wills, for every promise is a bondage to those that make a conscience to keep their promise, besides, it is not only variety that pleaseth women, but new changes, for stale acquaintance is as unpleasant as want of change, and the only hopes I have to the end of my suit, is, that I am a stranger and unknown, for women fancy men beyond what they are when unknown, and prize them less that their merits deserve, when they are acquainted.

MONSIEUR COMERADE   Well, we will not stay, but we will do our endeavour to get admittance.

Exeunt.

SCENE 25

Enter Madam Passionate as very ill, sitting in a chair groaning,
Enter Madam Jantil as to see her.

MADAM JANTIL   Madam, how do you find your health?

MADAM PASSIONATE   Very bad, for I am very ill, but I wonder at your fortitude, that you can bear such a cross as the loss of your husband so patiently.

MADAM JANTIL   O madam I am like those that are in a dropsy, their face seems full and fat, but their liver is consumed, and though my sorrow appears not outwardly, yet my heart is dead within me.

MADAM PASSIONATE   But your young years are a cordial to restore it, and a new love will make it as healthful as ever it was.

Enter Doll Pacify the Lady Passionate's maid,
with a porringer of caudle.[1]

DOLL PACIFY   Pray madam eat something, or otherwise you will kill yourself with fasting, for you have not eaten any thing since the beginning of your sorrow.

MADAM PASSIONATE   O carry that caudle away, carry it away, for the very sight doth overcome my stomach.

DOLL PACIFY   Pray madam eat but a little.

MADAM PASSIONATE   I care not for it, I cannot eat it, nor will not eat it: wherefore carry it away, or I will go away.

Both the ladies go out.

Enter Nell Careless Madam Jantil's Maid.

NELL CARELESS   Prithee if thy lady will not eat this caudle, give it me, for I have an appetite to it; but I wonder you will

---

1   caudle] "A warm drink consisting of thin gruel, mixed with wine or ale, sweetened and spiced, given chiefly to sick people, esp. women in childbed; also to their visitors" *(OED).*

offer your lady any thing to eat, but rather you should give her something to drink, for I have heard sorrow is dry, but never heard it was hungry.

DOLL PACIFY   You are mistaken, for sorrow is sharp, and bites upon the stomach, which causes an eager appetite.

NELL CARELESS   I am sure weeping eyes make a dry throat.

She eats and talks between each spoonful.

DOLL PACIFY   But melancholy thoughts make a hungry stomach: but faith if thou wert a widow, by thy eating thou wouldst have another husband quickly.

NELL CARELESS   Do you think I would marry again.

DOLL PACIFY   Heaven forbid that a young woman should live a widow.

NELL CARELESS   Why, is it a sin for a young woman to live a widow?

DOLL PACIFY   I know not what it would be to you, but it would be a case of conscience to me if I were a widow.

NELL CARELESS   By thy nice conscience thou seem'st to be a Puritan.

DOLL PACIFY   Well, I can bring many proofs: but were it not a sin, it is a disgrace.

NELL CARELESS   Where lies the disgrace?

DOLL PACIFY   In the opinion of the world, for old maids and musty widows are like the plague shunned of by all men, which affrights young women so much, as by running from it they catch hold on whatsoever man they meet, without consideration of what of whom they are, by which many times they fall into poverty and great misery.

NELL CARELESS   You teach a doctrine, that to escape one mischief they fall on another, which is worse than the first; wherefore it were better to live a musty widow as you call them, than a miserable wife; besides, a man cannot intimately love a widow, because he will be a cuckold, as being made one by her dead husband, and so live in adultery, and so she live in sin herself by cuckolding both her husbands, having had two.

DOLL PACIFY   I believe if you were a widow you would be tempted to that sin.

NELL CARELESS   Faith but I should not, for should I commit that sin, I should deserve the hell of discontent.

DOLL PACIFY   Faith you would marry if you were young, and fair, and rich.

NELL CARELESS   Those you mention would keep me from marrying: for if any would marry me for the love of youth and beauty, they would never love me long, because time ruins both soon; and if any one should marry me merely for my riches, they would love my riches so well and so much as there would be no love left for me that brought it, and if my husband be taken prisoner by my wealth, I shall be made a slave.

DOLL PACIFY   No, not if you be virtuous.

NELL CARELESS   Faith there is not one in an age that takes a wife merely for virtue, nor values a wife any thing the more for being so; for poor Virtue sits mourning unregarded and despised, not any one will so much as cast an eye towards her, but all shun her as you say they do old maids or musty widows.

DOLL PACIFY   Although you plead excellently well for not marrying, yet I make no question but you would willingly marry if there should come a young gallant.

NELL CARELESS   What's that, a fool that spends all his wit and money on his clothes? or is it a gallant young man, which is a man enriched with worth and merit?

DOLL PACIFY   I mean a gallant both for bravery and merit.

NELL CARELESS   Nay, they seldom go both together.

DOLL PACIFY   Well, I wish to Heaven that Hymen would give thee a husband, and then that Pluto would quietly take him away to see whether you would marry again, O I long for that time.

NELL CARELESS   Do not long too earnestly, lest you should miscarry of your desires.

Enter Madam Passionate, whereat Nell Careless hearing her come,
she runs away.

MADAM PASSIONATE   Who was it that run away?

DOLL PACIFY   Nell Careless Madam Jantil's maid.

MADAM PASSIONATE   O that I could contract a bargain for
such an indifferent mind as her young lady hath, or that the
pleasures of the world could bury my grief.

DOLL PACIFY   There is no way for that madam, but to please
yourself still with the present times, gathering those fruits
of life that are ripe, and next to your reach, not to endanger
a fall by climbing too high, nor to stay for that which is
green, nor to let it hand whilst it is rotten with time, nor to
murmur for that which is blown down by chance, nor to
curse the weather of accidents for blasting the blossoms,
nor the birds and worms of death, which is sickness and
pain, for picking and eating the berries, for nature allows
them a part as well as you, for there is nothing in the world
we can absolutely possess to ourselves; for Time, Chance,
Fortune and Death, hath a share in all things, life hath the
least.

MADAM PASSIONATE   I think so, for I am weary of mine.

The lady goes out.

Enter a man.

MAN   Mistress Dorothy, there are two or three gentlemen that
desire to speak with one of the widows' maids, and you
belong to one.

DOLL PACIFY   Well, what is their business?

MAN   I know not, but I suppose they will only declare that to
yourself.

She goeth out, and enters again as meeting the gentlemen.

DOLL PACIFY   Gentlemen, would you speak with me?

MONSIEUR LA GRAVITY   Yes, for we desire you will help us to the honour of kissing your ladies' hands, thereon to offer our service.

DOLL PACIFY   Sir, you must excuse me, for the sign of widow-hood is not as yet hung out, mourning is not on, nor the scutcheons are not hung over the gate, but if you please to come two or three days hence I may do you some service, but now it will be to no purpose to tell my lady, for I am sure she will receive no visits.

Exeunt.

THE SECOND PART OF BELL IN CAMPO

ACT I

SCENE 1

Enter Doctor Comfort, and Doll Pacify.

DOLL PACIFY   Good Master priest go comfort my old lady.

DOCTOR COMFORT   If you will comfort me, I will strive to comfort her.

DOLL PACIFY   So we shall prove the crumbs of comfort.

DOCTOR COMFORT   But is my lady so sad still?

DOLL PACIFY   Faith today she hath been better than I have seen her, for she was so patient as to give order for blacks; but I commend the young lady Madam Jantil, who bears out the siege of sorrow most courageously, and on my conscience I believe will beat grief from the fort of her heart, and become victorious over her misfortunes.

DOCTOR COMFORT   Youth is a good soldier in the warfare of life, and like a valiant Cornet or Ensign, keeps the colours up, and the flag flying, in despite of the enemies, and were our lady as young as Madam Jantil, she would grieve less, but to lose an old friend after the loss of a young beauty is a double, nay a treble affliction, because there is little or no hopes to get another good husband, for though an old woman may get a husband, yet ten thousand to one but he will prove an enemy, or a devil.

DOLL PACIFY   It were better for my lady if she would marry again, that her husband should prove a devil than a mortal enemy, for you can free her from the one though not from the other, for at your words, the great devil will avoid or vanish, and you can bind the lesser devils in chains, and whip them with holy rods until they roar again.

DOCTOR COMFORT   Nay, we are strong enough for the devil at all times, and in all places, neither can he deceive us in any shape, unless it be in the shape of a young beauty, and then I confess he overcomes us, and torments our hearts in the fire of love, beyond all expression.

DOLL PACIFY   If I were a devil I would be sure to take a most beautiful shape to torment you, but my lady will torment me if I stay any longer here.

Exeunt.

SCENE 2

Enter two Gentlemen.

1 GENT.   Sir, you being newly come from the army, pray what news?

2 GENT.   I suppose you have heard how our army was forced to fight by the enemy's provocations, hearing the Lord General lay sick, whereupon the General's lady the Lady Victoria, caused her Amazonians to march towards the masculine army, and to entrench some half a mile distance therefrom, which when the masculine army heard thereof, they were very much troubled thereat, and sent a command for them to retreat back, fearing they might be a disturbance, so a destruction unto them by doing some untimely or unnecessary action; but the female army returned the masculine army an answer, that they would not retreat unless they were beaten back, which they did believe the masculine sex would not, having more honour than to fight with the female sex; but if the men were so base, they were resolved to stand upon their own defence; but if they would let them alone, they would promise them upon the honour of their words not to advance any nearer unto the masculine army, as long as the masculine army could assault their enemies, or defend themselves, and in this posture I left them.

Exeunt.

SCENE 3

Enter the Lady Victoria, and her Heroickesses.

LADY VICTORIA   Noble Heroickesses, I have intelligences that
the army of Reformation begins to flag, wherefore now or
never is the time to prove the courage of our sex, to get
liberty and freedom from the female slavery, and to make
ourselves equal with men: for shall men only sit in Honour's chair, and women stand as waiters by? shall only men
in triumphant chariots ride, and women run as captives by?
shall only men be conquerors, and women slaves? shall
only men live by fame, and women die in oblivion? no, no,
gallant heroicks raise your spirits to a noble pitch, to a
divine[1] height, to get an everlasting renown, and infinite
praises, by honourable, but unusual actions: for honourable
fame is not got only by contemplating thoughts which lie
lazily in the womb of the mind, and prove abortive, if not
brought forth in living deeds; but worthy Heroickesses, at
this time Fortune desires to be the midwife, and if the gods
and goddesses did not intend to favour our proceedings
with a safe deliverance, they would not have offered us so
fair and fit an opportunity to be the mothers of glorious
actions, and everlasting fame, which if you be so unnatural
to strangle in the birth by fearful cowardice, may you be
blasted with infamy, which is worse than to die and be forgotten; may you be whipped with the torturing tongues of
our own sex we left behind us, and may you be scorned
and neglected by the masculine sex, whilst other women
are preferred and beloved, and may you walk unregarded
until you become a plague to yourselves; but if you arm
with courage and fight valiantly, may men bow down and
worship you, birds taught to sing your praises, Kings offer
up their crowns unto you, and honour enthrone you in a
mighty power.

---

1   divine] deaticall F1

May time and destiny attend your will,
Fame be your scribe to write your actions still;
And may the gods each act with praises fill.

ALL THE WOMEN   Fear us not, fear us not, we dare and will
follow you wheresoever and to what you dare or will lead
us, be it through the jaws of Death.

THE PRAYER

LADY VICTORIA   Great Mars thou god of war, grant that our
squadrons may like unbroken clouds move with entire
bodies, let courage be the wind to drive us on, and let our
thick swelled army darken their sun of hope with black
despair, let us pour down showers of their blood, to quench
the fiery flames of our revenge.

And where those showers fall, their deaths as seeds
Sown in Time's memory sprout up our deeds;
And may our acts triumphant garlands make,
Which Fame may wear for our heroicks' sake.

Exeunt.

SCENE 4

Enter Doctor Comfort, and Doll Pacify.

DOCTOR COMFORT   Doll, how doth our lady since the bury-
ing of my patron?
DOLL PACIFY   Faith she begins now to have regard to her
health, for she takes chocolate[1] every morning in her bed
fasting, and then she hath a mess of jelly broth for her
breakfast, and drinks a cup of sack before dinner, and eats a
white wine caudle every afternoon, and for her supper she
hath new laid eggs, and when she goes to bed, she drinks a

---

1   chocolate] Jackalato F1

hearty draught of Muscatel[1] to make her sleep well; besides, if she chances to wake in the night, she takes comfortable spirits, as Angelica, Aniseeds, Besor,[2] aqua mirabilis,[3] and the like hot waters, to comfort her heart, and to drive away all melancholy thoughts.

DOCTOR COMFORT   Those things will do it if it is to be done, but I am sorry that my lady hath sold all my patron's horses, saddles, arms, clothes, and such like things at the drum's head, and by outcries,[4] to get a little the more money for them, I fear the world will condemn her, as believing her to be covetous.

DOLL PACIFY   O that's nothing, for what she loses by being thought covetous, she will regain by being thought rich, for the world esteems and respects nothing so much as riches.

Exeunt.

---

1   Muscatel] Muskadine F1
2   Besor] Possibly a misspelling of "besom," identified in the OED as "Any agent that cleanses, purifies, or sweeps away things material or immaterial."
3   aqua mirabilis] Latin: "wonderful water," composed of a variety of spices distilled with alcohol. Intriguingly, Cavendish's reference predates the earliest entry for the word in the OED.
4   outcries] A seventeenth-century term for "auctions"; again, Cavendish's use of this term predates its earliest OED entry.

ACT II

SCENE 5

Enter two Gentlemen.

1 GENT. Pray sir what news from the army? You are newly come from thence.

2 GENT. I suppose you have heard how the effeminate army was some half a mile from the masculine armies; but the masculine army being very earnest to fight, not only to get victory and power, but to revenge each other's losses, as their friends slain in the former battle, which thoughts of revenge did so fire their minds and inflame their spirits, that if their eyes had been as much illuminated as their flaming spirits were, there might have been seen two blazing armies thus joining their forces against each other; at last began a cruel fight, where both the armies fought with such equal courages and active limbs, as for a long time neither side could get the better, but at last the army of Faction broke the ranks and files of the army of Reformation, whereupon every squadron began to fall into a confusion, no order was kept; no charge was heard, no command obey'd, terror and fear ran masked about, which helped to rout our army, whereupon the enemy kill'd many of our men, and wounded many more, and took numbers of prisoners; but upon this defeat came in the female army, in the time that some of the enemy was busy in gathering up the conquered spoils, others in pursuit of the remainders of our men, others were binding up the prisoners, others driving them to their quarters like a company of sheep to a market there to be sold; but when as the commanders perceived a fresh army coming towards them, their General commanded the trumpets to sound a retreat to gather them together, and also made haste to order and settle his men in battle array, and desirous their General was to have all the prisoners slain; but the female army came up so fast and so close to prevent that mischief, as they had not time to execute

that design; but their General encouraged his soldiers, and bid them not to be disheartened, persuading them not to lose what they had got from an army of men to an army of boys, for said he they seem to be no other by the appearance of their shapes and statures; but when the female army came to encounter them, they found their charge so hot and furious as made them give place, which advantage they took with that prudence and dexterity, as they did not only rout this army of Faction, killing and wounding many, and set their own countrymen at liberty, and recovered their losses, and gained many spoils, and took numbers of prisoners of their enemies with bag and baggage, but they pursued those that fled into their trenches, and beat them out of their works, and took possession thereof, where they found much riches; these trenches being taken, the Lady Victoria took possession, and made them her quarters, calling all her female soldiers to enter therein by the sound of flutes, which they always used instead of trumpets, and their drums were kettle-drums; but upon this victory the masculine sex of the army of Reformation was much out of countenance, being doubly or trebly overcome, twice by their enemy, and then by the gallant actions of the females which out-did them, yet they thought it best to take their advantage whilst the victory was fresh and flourishing, and their enemies weak and fearful, to lay siege to the next towns in the enemy's country; whereupon the Lady Victoria and her female soldiers hearing of the army of Reformation's designs, for they had sent the men to their own quarters as soon as the battle was won and victory got; also the masculine prisoners they sent to the men's quarters, not intermixing themselves with the men, but as I said they hearing the design they had to besiege the towns were much enraged for not making them of their councils, whereupon they sent a messenger like as an ambassador to tell the masculine army they did wonder at their ingratitude, that they should forget so much their relievers as to go upon any warlike design without making them acquainted therewith, striving as it were to steal the victory out of their hands, but said they, since we are become victorious over our enemies, and masters, and mistresses of the field, by our own valiant actions and prudent conducts, we will maintain our power by our own strengths, for our army is become now numerous, full and flourishing, formed, and conformable by our discipline, skillful by our practice, valiant by our resolutions, powerful by our victory, terrible to our enemies, honourable to our friends, and a subject of envy to the masculine sex; but your army is weak and decrepit, fitter for an hospital than for a field of war, your power is lost, your courage is cold, your discipline disordered,[1] and your command slighted, despised by your enemies, pitied by your friends, forsaken of good fortune, and made subject unto our effeminate sex, which we will use by our power like slaves. But when our Lord General who was recovered out of sickness, and all his commanders about him heard this message, which was delivered in full assembly, according as the Lady Victoria had commanded the message should be, the men could not choose but smile at the women's high and mighty words, knowing they had all sweet and gentle dispositions and complying natures, yet they were at a stand which to be pleased at most, as in hearing them disparage their masculine sex, or in advancing their own female sex by their self-commendations, but howsoever so well pleased the men were with the women's gallant actions, that every man was proud that had but a female acquaintance in the female army; but our Lord General was mightily taken with their bravadoes, and much mirth among the commanders was about it; but when they were to advise what to do in the affairs of war, and the warring women, the General told them he made no question but that most men knew by experience that women were won by gentle persuasions and fair promises, and not by rigid actions or angry frowns, besides said he, all noble natures strive to assist the weakest in all lawful actions, and that he was no gallant man that submits not to a woman in

---

1   disordered] disorderous F1

all things that are honourable, and when he doth dissent it must be in a courtly manner, and a complimentary[1] behaviour and expression, for that women were creatures made by nature, for men to love and admire, to protect and defend, to cherish and maintain, to seek and to sue to, and especially such women which have out-done all their sex, which nature ever made before them; wherefore said he, 'tis fit to these women above all others we should yield ourselves prisoners, not only in love but in arms; wherefore let us treat fairly with them, and give them their own conditions. But in the mean time the Lady Victoria thought it best not to lose any opportunity with talking out the time, wherefore she besieged a considerable fort, a place which was as it were the key that unlocked the passage into the heart of the enemy's kingdom, and at this siege they were when I came away, but the General and his council had sent a messenger unto them, but what his message was I cannot give you an account.

Exeunt.

SCENE 6

Enter two men in mourning.

1 MAN   Now my lord is entombed, our lady will enanchor[2] herself by his ashes.

2 MAN   'Tis strange so young and beautiful a lady should bury herself from the world, and quit all the pleasures thereof, to live with dead ashes.

1 MAN   A grieved mind, melancholy thoughts, and an oppressed heart, considers not the body, nor the world.

2 MAN   But yet I think 'tis an example that few of her sex will imitate.

---

1   complimentary] Complemental F1
2   enanchor]Become an anchorite, a religious recluse.

1 MAN   Because few of the female sex can truly grieve or be melancholy.

2 MAN   No, it is that few of the female sex can truly and constantly love.

Exeunt.

SCENE 7

The tomb being thrust on the stage, enter Madam Jantil and a company of mourners, but the Lady Jantil was attired in a garment of rich cloth of gold girt loosely about her, and a mantle of crimson velvet lined with powdered ermines over that, her woman bearing up the train thereof being long, her hair all unbound hung loose upon her shoulders and back, upon her head a rich crown of jewels, as also pendant jewels in her ears, and on her wrists costly bracelets; when she came in she goeth towards the tomb, and bows with great respect and devotion thereto, then speaks, directing her speech to every several figure.*

LADY JANTIL   Pallas and Mercury at thy death mourned,
So as to marble statues here th'are turned;
Mars sheaths his sword, and begs of thee a room,
To bury all his courage in thy tomb;
Hymen amazed stands, and is in doubt,
Thy death her¹ holy fire hath put out;
What various shapes of Fortune thou didst meet,
Thou scorn'st her frowns and kicks her with thy feet,
Now sound aloud the trumpet of good Fame,
And blow abroad his everlasting name.

---

*These following verses or speeches were written by my Lord Marquiss of Newcastle.
    [Cavendish's note]

1   her] his F1

After this she directs her speech to the outward figures
about the tomb.

The Cardinal Virtues pillars of thy fame,
Weep to see now each but an empty name
Only for painters and for carvers be,
When thy life sustain'd them more than they thee;
Each capital a sadder Virtue bears,
But for the Graces would be drowned in tears;
Faith strengthens Fortitude lest she should faint,
Hope comforts Prudence as her only saint;
And Charity to Justice doth advance
To counsel her, as Patience Temperance;
But woeful counselors they are each one,
Since grief for thy death turn'd them all to stone.

Then putting off her rich garments and ornaments
before mentioned as she was undressing
she spake thus.

Now I depose myself, and here lay down,
Titles, not honour, with my richer crown;
This crimson velvet mantle I throw by,
There ease and plenty in rich ermines lie;
Off with this glittering gown which once did bear
Ambition and fond pride lie you all there;
Bracelets and pendants which I now do wear,
Here I divest my arms and so each ear;
Cut off these dangling tresses once a crime,
Urging my glass to look away my time;
Thus all these worldly vanities I wave,
And bury them all in my husband's grave.

After this she calls for her other garments, which were a pure
white light silk loose garment, girt about her with a white
silk cord, and then puts on a thin black veil over it, and then

takes a book in her hand, but speaks as they were a
*putting on those latter garments.**

LADY JANTIL   Put on that pure and spotless garment white,
To show my chaster thoughts, my soul's delight;
Cord of humility about my waist,
A veil of obscure mourning about me cast;
Here by this sadder tomb shall be my station,
And in this book my holy contemplation.

She turns herself to her Servants.

Farewell my servants, farewell every one,
As you all love me pray leave me alone.

They all go forth weeping.

When they were all gone and she alone,
she turns herself to the tomb.

No dust shall on thy marble ever stay,
But with my sadder sighs I'll blow't away;
And the least spot that any pillar bears,
I'll wash it clean with grief of dropping tears;
Sun fly this hemisphere, and feast my eyes,
With melancholy night, and never rise,
Nor by reflection, for all light I hate,
Therefore no planet do illuminate;
The twinkling stars that in cold nights are seen,
Clouds muster up and hide them as a screen,
The centric fire raise vapours from the earth,
Get and be midwife for those fogs their birth;
Then chilling colds freeze up thy pores without,
That trembling earthquakes no where may get out;
And that our mother Earth may nothing wear,

---

* More of my Lord Marquess's, are these. [Cavendish's note]

But snow and icicles to curl her hair;
And so Dame Nature barren nothing bring,
Wishing a chaos, since despairs a spring;
Since all my joys are gone, what shall I do,
But wish the whole world ruined with me too?*

Exit.[1]

---

* Here ends my Lord Marquess's verses. [Cavendish's note]

---

1   Exit] Exeunt F1

ACT III

SCENE 8

*Enter the Lady Victoria, and many of her Amazons,
then enters a messenger from the masculine army.*

MESSENGER   May it please your Excellence, our Lord General
and the rest of the commanders have sent you and your
heroicks a letter, desiring it may be read in a full assembly.
LADY VICTORIA   One of you take the letter and read it.

*One of the women takes the letter
and reads it to all the company.*

THE LETTER

To the most excellent of her sex, and her most worthy
Heroickesses.
You goddesses on Earth, who have the power and domin-
ion over men, 'tis you we worship and adore, we pray and
implore your better opinions of us, than to believe we are
so unjust as to take the victory out of your fair hands, or so
vainglorious as to attribute it to ourselves, or so ungrateful
as not to acknowledge our lives and liberties from your valours, wisdoms, and good fortune, or so imprudent as to
neglect your power, or so ill-bred as to pass by you without
making our addresses, or so foolish as to go about any
action without your knowledge, or so unmannerly as to do
anything without your leave; wherefore we entreat you and
pray you to believe that we have so much honour in us, as
to admire your beauties, to be attentive to your discourses,
to dote on your persons, to honour your virtues, to divulge
your sweet graces, to praise your behaviours, to wait your
commands, to obey your directions, to be proud of your
favours, and we wear our lives only for your service, and
believe we are not only taken captives by your beauties, but
that we acknowledge we are bound as your slaves by your

valours; wherefore we all pray that you may not misinterpret our affections and care for[1] your persons, in believing we sent you away for your safety, for Heaven knows your departure was our Hell, and your absence our torments; but we confess our errors, and do humbly beg our pardons, for if you had accompanied us in our battles, you had kept us safe, for had we fought in your presence, our enemies had never overcome us, since we take courage from your eyes, life from your smiles, and victory from your good wishes, and had become conquerors by your encouragements, and so we might have triumphed in your favours, but hereafter your rules shall be our methods, yet give us leave humbly to offer our advice as subjects to their Princess if you think fit, we think it best to follow close the victory, lest that our enemies recruit their forces, with a sufficient strength to beat us out of what we have gained, or at least to hinder and oppose our entrance, and hopes of conquering them, where if you will give us leave we will besiege and enter their towns, and raze their walls down to the ground, which harbour their disorders, offending their neighbours' kingdoms; yet we are not so ambitious as to desire to be commanders, but to join our forces to yours, and to be your assistants, and as your common soldiers; but leaving all these affairs of war to your discretion, offering ourselves to your service,
We kiss your hands, and take our leaves for this time.

All the women fall into a great laughter,
ha, ha, ha, ha.

LADY VICTORIA   Noble Heroickesses, by your valours, and constant, and resolute proceedings, you have brought your tyrants to be your slaves; those that commanded your absence, now humbly sue your presence, those that thought you a hindrance have felt your assistance, the time is well altered since we were sent to retreat back from the

---

1   for] to F1

masculine army; and now nothing to be done in that army without our advice, with an humble desire they may join their forces with ours: but gallant Heroickesses, by this you may perceive we were as ignorant of ourselves as men were of us, thinking ourselves shiftless, weak, and unprofitable creatures, but by our actions of war we have proved ourselves to be every way equal with men; for what we want of strength, we have supplied by industry, and had we not done what we have done, we should have lived in ignorance and slavery.

ALL THE FEMALE COMMANDERS   All the knowledge of ourselves, the honour of renown, the freedom from slavery, and the submission of men, we acknowledge from you; for you advised us, counseled us, instructed us, and encouraged us to those actions of war: wherefore to you we owe our thanks, and to you we give our thanks.

LADY VICTORIA   What answer will you return to the masculine army?

ALL THE COMMANDERS   What answer you will think best.

LADY VICTORIA   We shall not need to write back an answer, for this messenger may deliver it by word of mouth; wherefore sir pray remember us to your General and his commanders, and tell them, that we are willing upon their submissions to be friends, and that we have not neglected our good fortune, for we have laid siege to so considerable a fort, which if taken, may give an easy passage into the kingdom, which fort we will deliver to their forces when they come, that they may have the honour of taking it; for tell them, we have got honour enough in the battle we fought, and victory we did win.

Exeunt.

SCENE 9

Enter Monsieur la Gravity, Monsieur Compagnion,
and Monsieur Comerade.

MONSIEUR COMPAGNION   We are bound to curse you Monsieur Gravity, for retarding our visits to the widows, for I told you we should come too late if we did not go before their husbands were buried.

MONSIEUR LA GRAVITY   But I do not hear they have made a promise to marry any as yet.

MONSIEUR COMPAGNION   That's all one unto us, but the noblest, youngest, richest, and fairest widow is gone; for though she is not promised or married, yet she is encloistered, and that is worse than marriage; for if she had been married there might have been some way or other Death would have found to have taken him away.

MONSIEUR COMERADE   Let us comfort ourselves with hopes, that it is but a lady's humour, which she will be soon weary of, for when her melancholy fit is over, she will come forth of her cloister, and be fonder to marry than if she had never gone in.

MONSIEUR LA GRAVITY   Well, since she is gone, let us assault the other.

MONSIEUR COMPAGNION   What, the old woman that hath never a tooth in her head?

MONSIEUR COMERADE   Why, she is rich, and she will kiss the softer for having no bones in her mouth.

MONSIEUR COMPAGNION   The devil shall kiss her before I will; besides, an old woman is thought a witch.

MONSIEUR LA GRAVITY   Pish, that is because they are grown ill-favoured with age, and all young people think whatsoever is ill-favoured belongs to the devil.

MONSIEUR COMPAGNION   An ancient man is a comely sight, being grave and wise by experience, and what he hath lost in his person, he hath gained in his understanding; besides, beauty in men looks as unhandsome as age in women, as being effeminate; but an old woman looks like the picture of envy, with hollow eyes, fallen cheeks, lank sides, black pale complexion, and more wrinkles than time hath minutes.

MONSIEUR COMERADE   Nay by your favour, some old women look like the full moon, with a red, swell'd, great, broad face, and their bodies like as a spongy cloud, thick and gross, like our fat hostess.

MONSIEUR LA GRAVITY   Gentlemen, why do you rail against ancient women so much, since those that are wise will never marry such boys as you?

MONSIEUR COMPAGNION   It is to be observed, that always old girls match themselves with young boys.

MONSIEUR LA GRAVITY   None but fools will do so.

MONSIEUR COMPAGNION   Why did you or any man else ever know a wise old woman, or a chaste young woman in their lives? for the one dotes with age, the other is corrupted with flattery, which is a bawd to self-conceit.

MONSIEUR LA GRAVITY   Grant it be so, yet it is better to marry an old doting fool, than a wanton young filly.

MONSIEUR COMPAGNION   For my part, I think now it is the best way to marry none, since Madam Jantil is gone, but to live like the Lacedaemonians,[1] all in common.

MONSIEUR LA GRAVITY   I am of another opinion, wherefore if you will go along with me to the old widow Madam Passionate, and help to countenance my suit, I shall take it as an act of friendship.

MONSIEUR COMERADE   Come, we will be thy pillars to support thee.

Exeunt.

---

1   Lacedaemonians] Spartans, inhabitants of the warrior city-state that often rivaled Athens.

SCENE 10

Enter Nell Careless, and Doll Pacify.

DOLL PACIFY What, doth thy lady resolve to live an anchorite?

NELL CARELESS I think so.

DOLL PACIFY How doth she pass away her time in her solitary cell?

NELL CARELESS Why, as soon as she rises she goeth to my lord's tomb, and says her prayers, then she returns and eats some little breakfast, as a crust of bread and a draught of water, then she goeth to her gallery and walks and contemplates all the forenoon, then about twelve o'clock at noon she goeth to the tomb again and says more prayers, then returns and eats a small dinner of some spoon-meats, and most of the afternoon she sits by the tomb and reads, or walks in the cloister, and views the pictures of my lord that are placed upon the walls, then in the evening she says her evening prayers at the tomb, and eats some light supper, and then prays at the tomb before she goeth to bed, and at midnight she rises and takes a white waxen torch lighted in her hand, and goeth to the tomb to pray, and then returns to bed.

DOLL PACIFY Faith she prays often enough in the day, she shall not need to pray at midnight; but why doth she rise just at midnight?

NELL CARELESS I know not, unless she is of that opinion which some have been of, which is that the souls or spirits of the dead rise at that hour out of their graves and tombs, to visit the face of the Earth, and perhaps my lady watches or hopes to converse by that means with my lord's ghost: for since she cannot converse with him living, she desires to converse with him dead, or otherwise she would not spend most of her time at this tomb as she doth; but how doth thy lady spend her time now?

DOLL PACIFY Faith as a lady should do, with nourishing her body with good hearty meats and drink. And though my lady doth not pray at midnight, yet she converses with spirits at that time of night.

NELL CARELESS   What spirits?

DOLL PACIFY   Marry spirits distilled from wine and other cordials, which she drinks when she wakes, which is at midnight; but do you watch fast and pray as thy lady doth?

NELL CARELESS   No truly, for I feed with the rest of my lady's servants, which live within the house without the cloister, and they eat and drink more liberally.

Exeunt.

SCENE 11

Enter Monsieur la Gravity, Monsieur Compagnion, and Monsieur Comerade, as to Madam Passionate's house; Enter Madam Passionate's gentleman usher.

MONSIEUR LA GRAVITY   Sir, we come to kiss the hands of the Lady Passionate, if you please to inform your lady of us.

GENTLEMAN USHER   I shall, if't please you to enter into another room.

Exeunt.

SCENE 12

Enter Doll Pacify, as to her lady Madam Passionate in her chamber where her cabinets were.

DOLL PACIFY   Madam, there are three gentlemen come to visit you, desiring you would give them leave to kiss your hands.

MADAM PASSIONATE   Shut down the lid of the cellar[1] of

---

1   cellar] Seller F1

strong-waters, and rid away the loose things that lie about, that my chamber may appear in some order.

The maid sets things in order, whilst the old lady is trimming herself in the looking-glass.

MADAM PASSIONATE   Bring in those gentlemen.[1]

*The maid goes out, then enters with the gentlemen;
the two young men speak to each other
the time that Monsieur la Gravity
is saluting.*

MONSIEUR COMPAGNION   Ay, marry sir, here is a comfortable smell indeed.
MONSIEUR COMERADE   Faith the smell of these spirits overcomes my spirits, for I am ready to swoon.

Then they go and salute the lady.

MADAM PASSIONATE   Pray gentlemen sit down.

They sit.

Truly I have had so great a wind in my stomach as it hath troubled me very much.

Compagnion speaks softly to Comerade.

MONSIEUR COMPAGNION   Which to express the better, she rasps at every word to make a full stop.
MONSIEUR LA GRAVITY   Perchance madam you have eaten some meat that digests not well.
MONSIEUR COMPAGNION [*aside*]   A toad.
MADAM[2] PASSIONATE   No, truly I cannot guess what should

---

1   gentlemen.] Gentlemen? F1
2   Madam] Lady F1

cause it, unless it be an old pippin,[1] and that is accounted a great restorative.

She fetches a great sigh.

But I believe it is the drugs of my sorrow which stick in my stomach: for I have grieved mightily for my dead husband rest his soul; he was a good man, and as kind a husband as ever woman had.

MONSIEUR LA GRAVITY   But the destinies madam are not to be controlled, death seizes on all, be it early or late; wherefore every one is to make their life as happy as they can, since life is so short; and in order to [do] that, you should choose a new companion to live withal; wherefore you must marry again.

LADY PASSIONATE   'Tis true, the Destinies are not to be controlled as you say, wherefore if my destiny be to marry, I shall marry, or else I shall die a widow.

MONSIEUR COMPAGNION [*aside, as in Comerade's ear*]   She will lay the fault of her second marriage on Destiny, as many the like foolish actions are laid to Destiny's charge, which she was never guilty of.

MONSIEUR LA GRAVITY   If I should guess at your destiny, I should judge you will marry again, by the quickness of your eyes which are fair and lovely.

She simpers.

LADY PASSIONATE   O sir you flatter me.

MONSIEUR COMPAGNION [*aside*]   I'll be sworn that he doth.

LADY PASSIONATE   But my eyes were good, as I have been told, both by my glass and friends, when I was young, but now my face is in the autumnal.

MONSIEUR COMPAGNION [*aside to Comerade*]   Nay faith, it is in the midst of winter.

---

1   pippin] A kind of apple; ironically, this "great restorative" is probably as wrinkled as Madam Passionate herself, as the snide asides of her suitors suggest.

LADY PASSIONATE   But now you talk of eyes, that young gentleman's eyes (points to Compagnion) do so resemble my husband's as I can scarce look off from them, they have a good aspect.

MONSIEUR COMPAGNION   I am glad they have an influence upon your Ladyship.

She speaks as softly to herself.

MADAM PASSIONATE[1]   By my faith wittily answered, I dare say he is a noble youth.
Sir, for resemblance of he who[2] is dead, I shall desire your continued acquaintance.

Compagnion softly to Comerade.

MONSIEUR COMPAGNION   She woos me with her husband's dead skull.
I shall render my service to your Ladyship.

She bows him thanks with simpering and smiling countenance, and a bridled head.

Monsieur la Gravity softly to himself.

MONSIEUR LA GRAVITY   Those young youths I perceive will be my ruin if not prevented. Madam, will your Ladyship honour me so much as to give me the private hearing of a few words.

LADY PASSIONATE   Yes sir.

She removes with him a little space.

MONSIEUR LA GRAVITY   Madam, although I am not such a one as I could wish myself for your sake, yet I am a gentle-

---

1   Madam Passionate] La. Passion. F1
2   he who] him which F1

man, and what I want in person or estate, my affection, respect, and tender regard to your person, worth, and merit shall make good; besides madam, my years suiting to your Ladyship's will make the better agreement in marriage.

LADY PASSIONATE Sir you must excuse me; for though you merit a better wife than I, yet I cannot answer your affections; wherefore I desire you will desist in your suit, for I am resolved, if I do marry, to please my fancy.

MONSIEUR LA GRAVITY If your Ladyship cannot love me, Heaven forbid I should marry you; wherefore I wish your Ladyship such a husband as you can fancy best and love most.

They return to the two other gentlemen,
they all take their leaves.

Madam, your most humble servant.

They go through the stage, and come upon in again,
as it were at the street door.

MONSIEUR LA GRAVITY Where is our coach?

Enter a Footman.

Call the coach to the door.[1]

Enter Doll Pacify as from her lady
to Monsieur Compagnion.

DOLL PACIFY Sir, pray give me leave to speak a word or two with you.

MONSIEUR COMPAGNION As many as you please.

DOLL PACIFY Sir, my lady desires your company tomorrow to dinner, but she desires you will come alone.

MONSIEUR COMPAGNION Pray give your lady thanks for her

---

1 door] Door? F1

favours, and tell her if I can possibly I will wait on her
Ladyship.

Doll Pacify goes out.

MONSIEUR COMERADE   Now what encouragement have you
from the old lady?

MONSIEUR COMPAGNION   Faith so much as I am ashamed of
it, for she invites me to come alone.

MONSIEUR COMERADE   On my life if thou wilt not woo her,
she will woo thee.

MONSIEUR COMPAGNION   Like enough; for there is nothing
so impudent as an old woman, they will put a young man
be he never so debauched[1] out of countenance.

MONSIEUR COMERADE   But faith consider of it, for she is
rich.

MONSIEUR COMPAGNION   So is the devil, as poets say, Pluto
the god of riches.

MONSIEUR COMERADE   I grant it, and is not he best served?
For every one bows with respect, nay worships and adores
riches, and they have reason so to do, since all are miserable
that have it not, for poverty is a torment beyond all suffer-
ance, which causes many to hang themselves, either in the
chain of infamy, or in a hempen rope, or to do an act[2]
against the strict laws of a commonwealth which is to
commit self-murder; besides, poverty is the slave and
drudge, the scorn and reproach of the world, & it makes all
younger brothers sharks, and mere cheats, whereas this old
lady's riches will not only give you an honest mind, and
create noble thoughts, but will give you an honourable
reputation in the world: for every one will think you wise
although you were a fool, valiant although you were a
coward, and you shall have the first offers of all offices, and
all officers will be at your devotion, they will attend you as
slaves, the lawyers will plead on your side, and judges will

---

1   debauched] deboist F1
2   an act] acts F1

give sentence according as you desire, courtiers will flatter you, and divines will pray for you in their pulpits, and if your old lady die, and leave you her wealth, you shall have all the young beautiful virgins in the kingdom gather to that city, town, or village where you live, omitting no art that may prefer them to your affection.

MONSIEUR COMPAGNION   You say well, and I could approve of your counsel, if she would die soon after I had married her.

MONSIEUR COMERADE   Why, put the case she should live a great while, as the truth is old women are tough, and endure long, yet you will have her estate to please yourself withal, which estate will buy you fine horses, great coaches, maintain servants and great retinues to follow you.

MONSIEUR COMPAGNION   But she is so devilish old.

MONSIEUR COMERADE   Why, let her keep her age to herself, whilst you keep a young mistress to yourself, and it is better to have an old wife that will look after your family, and be careful and watchful therein, and a young mistress, than a young wife, which will be a tyrannical mistress, which will look after nothing but vanities, and love servants, whilst you poor wretch look like a contented cuckold, and so out of countenance as you dare not show your face, whilst she spends your estate running about with every vain idle fellow to plays, masks, balls, exchanges, taverns, or meets at a private friend's private lodging, also making great feasts and entertainments, where after dinner and supper, there must be gaming at cards and dice; where for her honour, or at least seeming so, to lose five hundred or a thousand pounds away, and when they rise with or from their losses, singing with a feigned voice, as if it were a trifle not to be considered or considerable, thus if you marry an old and rich lady you may live and spend her estate, but if you marry for youth and beauty, your wife will live and spend your estate; besides, the husband of an old lady lives like the great Turk, having a seraglio,[1] but marrying a

---

1   seraglio] A harem.

young wife you live like a prisoner never durst show your head.

MONSIEUR LA GRAVITY He gives you good counsel, and let me advise you to go to this lady as she hath invited you, for I perceive she hath a young tooth in her old head by refusing me, and there is none so fit to pull it out as you are, wherefore go.

MONSIEUR COMPAGNION Well gentlemen, I will try if my reason and your counsel can prevail in my choice.

Exeunt.

ACT IV

SCENE 13

*Enter Madam Jantil in her habit with a white taper lighted in her
hand, the tomb being thrust upon the stage she goeth to the tomb,
then kneels down and seems as praying, after that she rises,
holding out the torch with the other hand
speaks as follows.**

MADAM JANTIL   Welcome sad thoughts that're[1] heapt up
    without measure,
They're joys to me and wealthy sons of treasure;
Were all my breath turn'd into sighs 'twould ease me,
And showers of tears to bathe my griefs would please me;
Then every groan so kind to take my part,
To vent some sorrows still thus from my heart;
But there's no vacuum, O my heart is full,
As it vents sorrows new griefs in doth pull;
Is there no comfort left upon the Earth?
Let me consider vegetable birth;
The new born virgin lily of the day,
In a few hours dies, withers away;
And all the odoriferous flow'rs that're sweet,
Breathe but a while, and then with Death do meet;
The stouter oak at last doth yield, and must
Cast his rough skin and crumble all to dust;
But what do sensitives? Alas they be,
Beasts, birds and flesh to die as well as we;
And harder minerals though longer stay
Here for a time, yet at the last decay,
And die as all things else that're in this world,
For into Death's arms every thing is hurled;
Alas poor man thou'rt in the worst estate,

---

* These verses being written by my Lord, the Marquess of Newcastle. [Cavendish's
  note]

---

1 that're] that's F1

Thou diest as these, yet an unhappier fate;
Thy life's but trouble still of numerous passions,
Torments thyself in many various fashions;
Condemn'd thou art to vexing thoughts within;
When beasts both live and die without a sin;
O happy beasts that grazing look no higher,
Or are [not] tormented with thought's flaming fire;
Thus by myself and other still annoyed,
And made o'purpose but to be destroyed
Poor Man.*

*Muses some short time,
then kneels to the tomb again and prays as to herself, then rises and
bows to the tomb, so Exit.*

SCENE 14

Enter two Gentlemen.

1 GENT. What news sir of our armies abroad?
2 GENT. Why sir thus, in the time of our masculine army's
  recruiting, the female army had taken the fort they
  besieged, whereupon the taking of that fort, many considerable towns and strongholds surrendered, and submitted
  to the female army; whereupon the Lady Victoria sent to
  her husband to bring his army, when the General and all
  the masculine army came to the female army, much mirth
  and jesting there was betwixt the heroicks and heroickesses, and so well they did agree, as the female army feasted
  the masculine army, and then gave the possession of the
  surrendered towns to the Lord General, and the Lady
  Victoria, and all her army kept themselves in and about the
  fort, laying all their victorious spoils therein, and whilst the
  masculine army is gone to conquer the Kingdom of

---

* Here ends my Lord Marquesses verses. [Cavendish's note]

Faction, they stay there upon the frontiers, passing their time in heroic sports, as hunting the stags, wild boars, and the like, and those that have the good fortune to kill the chase, is brought to the fort and trenches in triumph, and is Queen until another chase is kill'd; but we hear the masculine army goeth on with victorious success.

1 GENT.   I am very glad to hear it.

Exeunt.

SCENE 15

Enter Doll Pacify, and Nell Careless.

NELL CARELESS   O Doll, I hear thy lady is married, and not only married, but she hath married a very young man, one that might be her grandson, or son at least.

DOLL PACIFY   Yes, yes, my lady doth not intend to live with the dead as your lady doth, but to have the company and pleasure of that which hath most life, which is a young man.

NELL CARELESS   Her marriage was very sudden.

DOLL PACIFY   So are all unconsidered[1] marriages, but happy is the wooing that is not long a-doing.

NELL CARELESS   If I had been your lady, I would have prolonged the time of my wooing, for the wooing time is the happiest time.

DOLL PACIFY   Yes, if she had been as young as you or your lady, but time bids my lady make haste.

Exeunt.

---

1   unconsidered] inconsiderated F1

SCENE 16

Enter two Gentlemen.

1 GENT.   Do you hear the news.

2 GENT.   What news?

1 GENT.   Why, the news is that all the Kingdom of Faction
hath submitted to the Kingdom of Reformation, and that
the armies are returning home.

2 GENT.   I am glad of it.

Exeunt.

SCENE 17

Enter Madam Passionate alone.

MADAM PASSIONATE   O unfortunate woman that I am, I was
rich, and lived in plenty, none to control me, I was mistress
of my self, estate and family, all my servants obeyed me,
none durst contradict me, but all flattered me, filling my
ears with praises, my eyes with their humble bows and
respectful behaviours, devising delightful sports to entertain my time, making delicious meats to please my palate,
sought out the most comfortable drinks to strengthen and
increase my spirits, thus did I live luxuriously, but now I am
made a slave, and in my old age which requires rest and
peace, which now Heaven knows I have but little of, for
the minstrels keep me waking, which play whilst my husband and his whores dance, and he is not only contented to
live riotously with my estate, but sits amongst his wenches
and rails on me, or else comes and scoffs at me to my face;
besides, all my servants slight and neglect me, following
those that command the purse, for this idle young fellow
whom I have married first seized on all my goods, then let
leases for many lives out of my lands, for which he had
great fines, and now he cuts down all my woods, and sells

all my lands of inheritance, which I foolishly and fondly delivered by deed of gift, the first day I married, divesting myself of all power, which power had I kept in my own hands I might have been used better, whereas now when he comes home drunk, he swears and storms, and kicks me out of my warm bed, and makes me sit shivering and shaking in the cold, whilst my maid takes my place; but I find I cannot live long, for age and disorders bring weakness and sickness, and weakness and sickness bring death, wherefore my marriage bed is like to prove my grave, whilst my husband's curses are my passing bell, hey ho.

Exit.

SCENE 18

Enter two Gentlemen.

1 GENT.   I hear the army is returning home.

2 GENT.   Yes, for they are returned as far back as to the effeminate army, and all the masculine commanders have presented all the female commanders with their spoils got in the Kingdom of Faction, as a tribute to their heroic acts, and due for their assistance, and safety of their lives and country.

1 GENT.   And do not you hear what privileges and honours the King and his council have resolved and agreed upon to be given to the female army, and the honours particularly to be given the Lady Victoria?

2 GENT.   No.

1 GENT.   Why then I will tell you some, the Lady Victoria shall be brought through the city in triumph, which is a great honour, for never any one makes triumphs in a monarchy but the King himself; then that there shall be a blank for the female army to write their desires and demands; also there is an armour of gold and a sword a-making, the hilt being set with diamonds, and a chariot all

gilt and embroidered to be presented to the Lady Victoria, and the city is making great preparation against her arrival.

2 GENT.   Certainly she is a lady that deserves as much as can be given either from Kings, states, or poets.

Exeunt.

SCENE 19

Enter the Lady Jantil as being sick brought by two men in a chair, and set by the tomb of her dead lord, and many servants and friends about her weeping.

MADAM JANTIL   Where is my secretary?

SECRETARY   Here madam.

MADAM JANTIL   Read the will I caus'd you to write down.

THE WILL READ.

I Jantil the widow of Seigneur Valeroso, do here make a free gift of all these following.

Item, all my husband's horses and saddles and whatsoever belongs to those horses, with all his arms, pikes, guns, trumpets, colours, wagons, coaches, tents, and all he had belonging to the war, to be distributed amongst his officers of war, according to each degree, I freely give.

Item, all his library of books I give to that college he was a pupil in when he was at the university.

Item, to all his servants I give the sum of their yearly wages to be yearly paid them during their lives.

Item, I give two hundred pounds a year pension to his chaplain Doctor Educature during his life.

Item, I give a hundred pounds a year pension to his steward during his life.

Item, I give fifty pounds a year pension to his secretary during his life.

Item, I give a hundred pounds per annum, for the use and repair of this tomb of my dead husband's.

Item, I give a thousand pounds a year to maintain ten religious persons to live in this place or house by this tomb.

Item, I give three thousand pounds to enlarge the house, and three thousand pounds more to build a chapel by my husband's tomb.

Item, Two hundred pounds a year I give for the use and repair of the house and chapel.

Item, I give my maid Nell Careless a thousand pounds to live a single life.

Item, I give the rest of my estate which was left me by my husband Seigneur Valeroso to the next of his name.*

[MADAM] JANTIL   So 'tis well

O Death hath shaked me kindly by the hand,
To bid me welcome to the silent grave;
'Tis dead and numb sweet Death how thou dost court me,
O let me clap thy fallen cheeks with joy,
And kiss the emblem of what once was lips,
Thy hollow eyes I am in love withal,
And thy bald head beyond youth's best curl'd hair,
Prithee embrace me in thy colder arms,
And hug me there to fit me for thy mansion;
Then bid our neighbour worms to feast with us,
Thus to rejoice upon my holy day;
But thou art slow, I prithee hasten Death,
And linger not my hopes thus with thy stay,
'Tis not thy fault thou sayst, but fearful nature
That hinders thus Death's progress in his way;
Oh foolish Nature thinks't thou canst withstand,
Death's conquering and inevitable hand;
Let me have music for divertisement,
This is my masque, Death's ball, my soul to dance
Out of her frail and fleshly prison here;
Oh could I now dissolve and melt, I long

---

*These following speeches and songs of hers, my Lord the Marquis of Newcastle writ.
  [Cavendish's note]

To free my soul in slumbers with a song;
In soft and quiet sleep here as I lie,
Steal gently out O soul, and let me die.

Lies as asleep.

SONG

O you gods pure angels send her,
Here about to attend her;
Let them wait and here condole,
Till receive her spotless soul;
So serene it is and fair,
It will sweeten all the air;
You this holy wonder bear,
With the music of the spheres;
Her soul's journey in a trice,
You'll bring safe to paradise;
And rejoice the saints that say,
She makes Heaven's holiday.

The song ended she opens her eyes, then speaks.

[MADAM JANTIL] Death hath not finish'd yet his work, he's
   slow,
But he is sure, for he will do't at last;
Turn me to my dear lord, that I may breathe
My last words unto him, my dear,
Our marriage join'd our flesh and bone,
Contracted by those holy words made one;
But by our loves we join'd each other's hearts,
And vow'd that death should never us part;[1]
Now death doth marry us, since now we must,
Ashes to ashes be mingling one dust,
And our joyed souls in heaven married then,
When our frail bodies rise, we'll wed again;

---

1 part] depart F1

And now I am joyed to lie by thy lov'd side,
My soul with thy soul shall in Heaven reside.
For that is all my*

*In this last word she dies, which when her servants see, they cry out
she is dead, she is dead.*

Doctor Educature says that.

DOCTOR EDUCATURE   She is dead, she is dead, the body
   hence convey,
         And to our mistress our last rites we'll pay.

*So they lay her by her husband upon the tomb,
and drawing off the tomb go out.*

Exeunt.

---

*Here ends my Lord Marquesses writing. [Cavendish's note]

ACT V

SCENE 20

Enter citizens' wives and their apprentices.

1 CITIZEN'S WIFE   Where shall we stand to see this triumphing?

2 CITIZEN'S WIFE   I think neighbour this is the best place.

3 CITIZEN'S WIFE   We shall be mightily crowded there.

2 CITIZEN'S WIFE   For my part I will stand here, and my apprentice Nathaniel shall stand by me, and keep off the crowd from crowding me.

NATHANIEL   Truly Mistress that is more than I am able to do.

3 CITIZEN'S WIFE   Well neighbour if you be resolved to stand here, we will keep you company. Timothy stand by me.

TIMOTHY   If you stand here Mistress the squibs will run under your clothes.

3 CITIZEN'S WIFE   No matter Timothy, let them run where they will.

They take their stand.

1 CITIZEN'S WIFE   I hope neighbour none will stand before us, for I would not but see this Lady Victoria for anything, for they say she hath brought articles for all women to have as many husbands as they will, and all tradesmen's wives shall have as many apprentices as they will.

2 CITIZEN'S WIFE   The gods bless her for it.

Enter a crowd of people.

She is coming, she is coming.

Officers come.

Stand up close, make way.

Enter many prisoners which march by two and two, then enter
many that carry the conquered spoils, then enters the
Lady Victoria in a gilt chariot drawn with eight white horses,
four on abreast, the horses covered with cloth of gold,
and great plumes of feathers on their heads.

The Lady Victoria was adorned after this manner; she had a coat
on all embroidered with silver and gold, which coat reached no
further than the calves of her legs, and on her legs and feet she
had buskins and sandals embroidered suitable to her coat; on her
head she had a wreath or garland of laurel, and her hair curl'd
and loosely flowing, in her hand a crystal ball headed with gold
at each end, and after the chariot marched all her female officers
with laurel branches in their hands, and after them the inferior
she soldiers, then going through the stage, as through the city, and
so entering again, where on the midst of the stage as if it were the
midst of the city, the magistrates meet her, so her chariot makes a
stand, and one as the recorder speaks a speech to her.

[RECORDER]   Victorious lady, you have brought peace safety
and conquest to this kingdom by your prudent conduct
and valiant actions, which never any of your sex in this
kingdom did before you. Wherefore our gracious King is
pleased to give you that which was never granted nor given
to any before, which is to make you triumphant, for no
triumph is ever made in monarchies, but by the kings
thereof; besides our gracious King hath caused an act to be
made and granted to all your sex, which act I have order to
declare, as
First, that all women shall hereafter in this kingdom be
mistress in their own houses and families.
Secondly, they shall sit at the upper end of the table above
their husbands.
Thirdly, that they shall keep the purse.
Fourthly, they shall order their servants, turning from, or
taking into their service what number they will, placing
them how they will, and ordering how they will, and giving them what wages they will or think fit.

Fifthly, they shall buy in what provisions they will.

Sixthly, all the jewels, plate, and household furniture they shall claim as their own, and order them as they think good.

Seventhly, they shall wear what fashioned clothes they will.

Eighthly, they shall go abroad when they will, without control, or giving of any account thereof.

Ninthly, they shall eat when they will, and of what they will, and as much as they will, and as often as they will.

Tenthly, they shall go to plays, masques, balls, churchings, christenings, preachings, whensoever they will, and as fine and bravely attired as they will.

Lastly, that they shall be of their husbands' counsel.

*When those are read, all the women cry out, God save the King, God save the King, and Heaven reward the
Lady Victoria.*

Then an act was read concerning the Lady Victoria.

[RECORDER]   As for you most gallant lady, the King hath caused to be enacted that

First, all poets shall strive to set forth your praise.

Secondly, that all your gallant acts shall be recorded in story, and put in the chief library of the kingdom.

Thirdly, that your arms you fought in, shall be set in the King's armoury.

Fourthly, that you shall always wear a laurel garland.

Fifthly, you shall have place next to the King's children.

Sixthly, that all those women that have committed such faults as are a dishonour to the female sex, shall be more severely punished than heretofore, in not following your exemplary virtues, and all those who have followed your example shall have respective honour done to them by the state.

Seventhly and lastly, your figure shall be cast in brass, and then set in the midst of the city armed as it was in the day of battle.

The Lady Victoria rises up in her chariot, and then bows herself to the magistrates.

LADY VICTORIA   Worthy sir, the honour and privileges my gracious King and sovereign hath bestowed upon me, are beyond my merit.

Then was read the acts concerning the rest of the female army.

[RECORDER]   Our gracious King hath caused to be enacted, as First, all the chief female commanders shall have place, as every lord's wife shall take place of an earl's wife that hath not been a soldier in the army; every knight's wife before a baron's wife that hath not been a soldier in the army; an esquire's wife before a knight's wife; a doctor's wife before an esquire's wife that hath not been [a] soldier in the army; a citizen's wife before a doctor's wife; a yeoman's wife before a citizen's wife that hath not been a soldier in the army; and all tradesmen's wives that have been soldiers in the army shall be free in all the corporations in this kingdom, these acts during their lives, and all the chief commanders shall be presented according to their quality and merit.

> *All the female soldiers cried out,*
> *God save the King,*
> *God save the King.*

After this the Lady Victoria is drawn on her chariot, and the rest walk after all.

Exeunt.

SCENE 21

Enter Doll Pacify, and Nell Careless.

DOLL PACIFY   O Nell, I hear thy lady is dead, and hath left thee a thousand pounds.

Nell weeps.

NELL CARELESS   I wish my lady had liv'd, although I had begg'd all my life.

DOLL PACIFY   I am not of your mind, I had rather live well myself, as to live in plenty, than to live poor for the life of anybody, and if upon that condition my lady would leave me a thousand pounds, I care not if she died tomorrow; but my young master hath robbed me of all: but Nell, for all thou art left a thousand pounds, it is upon such a condition, as for my part, had it been to me, I should not thank the giver, for they say it is given thee upon condition to live a single life.

NELL CARELESS   Truly I have seen so much sorrow in my lady, and so much folly in your lady concerning husbands, that had not my lady enjoined me to live a single life, I would never have married; wherefore my lady's generosity did not only provide for my bodily life, and for my plentiful living, but provided for the tranquillity of my mind, for which I am trebly obliged to reverence her memory.

Exeunt.

SCENE 22

Enter two Gentlemen.

I GENT.   The Lady Victoria hath been at court, and hath had public audience.

2 GENT.   Yes, and the Lady Victoria and her she-officers and commanders have distributed all their spoils got in these wars amongst the common she-soldiers.

1 GENT.   All the ladies that went not with the army look most pitifully out of countenance.

2 GENT.   Yes, and they are much troubled that the heroicks shall take place.

1 GENT.   The Lord General seems to be very proud of his lady, methinks he looks upon her with a most pleased eye.

2 GENT.   He hath reason, for never man had so gallant and noble a lady, nor more virtuous and loving a wife than the Lord General hath.

Exeunt.

FINIS.

THE SOCIABLE COMPANIONS

TO THE READERS.

It is most certain, that those that perform public actions, expose themselves to public censures; and so do writers, live they never so privately and retired, as soon as they commit their works to the press. Which should persuade wise persons to be very cautious what they publish; especially in a malicious, and envious age. I do not say, that this is so; but if it be, I can truly say, that I am sorry of it, merely for the age's sake, and not in relation to myself, or my books; which I write and disperse abroad, only for my own pleasure, and not to please others: being very indifferent whether anybody reads them or not; or being read, how they are esteemed. For none but poor and mean spirits will think themselves concerned in spiteful censures. Having observed, that the most worthy and most meritorious persons have the most envious detractors, it would be a presumptuous opinion of me to imagine myself in danger to have any: but however, their malice cannot hinder me from writing, wherein consists my chiefest delight and greatest pastime; nor from printing what I write, since I regard not so much the present as future ages, for which I intend all my books.

When I call this new one, Plays, I do not believe to have given it a very proper title: for it would be too great a fondness to my works to think such plays as these suitable to ancient rules, in which I pretend no skill; or agreeable to the modern humour, to which I dare acknowledge my aversion: but having pleased my fancy in writing many dialogues upon several subjects, and having afterwards ordered them into acts and scenes, I will venture, in spite of the critics, to call them plays; and if you like them so, well and good; if not, there is no harm done: and so farewell.

THE ACTORS NAMES.

Master Save-all.
Captain Valour.
Lieutenant Fightwell.
Cornet[1] Defendant.
Will Fullwit.
Harry Sensible.
Dick Traveller.
Get-all, an Usurer.
Sergeant Plead-all, a Lawyer.
Doctor Cure-all, a Physician.
Roger and Tom, Get-all's two Men.
Two other Men, one the Sergeant's, the other the Doctor's.
A Drawer.
Mistress Peg Valourosa Sister to Captain Valour.
Mistress Jane Fullwit, Will Fullwit's Sister.
Mistress Anne Sensible, Harry Sensible's Sister.
Mistress Informer, an old decayed Gentlewoman.
Mistress Prudence, Daughter of Master Save-all.
Several Wooers, and Others.

PROLOGUE

Noble spectators. Our authoress doth say,
She doth believe you will condemn her play.
Here's no design, no plot, nor any ground,
Foundation none, not any to be found,
But like the world's globe it hath no support
But hangs by geometry: nor hath it fort
To make it strong, nor walls to keep out censure,
Yet she will valiantly stand the adventure.

---

1   Cornet] "The fifth commissioned officer in a troop of cavalry, who carried the
    colours; corresponding to the ensign in infantry" (*OED*).

THE SOCIABLE COMPANIONS; OR THE FEMALE WITS: A COMEDY

ACT I

SCENE I

Enter Colonel, Captain, Lieutenant.

COLONEL.   What News, Captain?

CAPTAIN.   It is old saying, that ill news hath wings, and good news no legs.

COLONEL.   Hath thy news wings, or no legs?

CAPTAIN.   It hath wings; for it is reported for certain, that the army shall be disbanded, and all the soldiers cashiered.

LIEUTENANT.   So then the army will be a flying army.

CAPTAIN.   But yet we must beg upon crutches.

LIEUTENANT.   I believe we should have been stronger, if we had been of any other profession, having had a better employment to have busied our minds and persons with; for soldiers for the most part, their time and lives are idle, having no great employment or business, but when they march or fight, which is not every day or week; and when we are in quarters or trenches, we have nothing to do but watch by turns; and therefore we are forced (for want of better employment) to pass our time with the wenches in the suburbs, or the baggages that follow the army, with whom we get the pox.

CAPTAIN.   But how shall our pocky[1] bodies live, if we be cashiered?

LIEUTENANT.   We must endeavour to get into some hospital for cure.

COLONEL.   That will be more difficult, than to get into a court for preferment, Lieutenant.

CAPTAIN.   The truth is, we may more easily get into a court,

---

1   pocky] Riddled with the pox, a form of venereal disease.

than to have a cure in an hospital; and we may more easily be cured in an hospital, than get preferment in a court; for soldiers are never regarded in time of peace; for when a war is ended, soldiers are out of credit.

COLONEL. And in time of war courtiers are out of fashion.

CAPTAIN. Faith, soldiers regard not new modes, no more than wars give to flattery.

LIEUTENANT. But courtiers do oftener turn soldiers, than soldiers courtiers.

COLONEL. Faith, Lieutenant, much alike; for courtiers are too weak to make soldiers, and soldiers are too rough to make courtiers.

LIEUTENANT. How, come courtiers weak, Colonel?

COLONEL. As soldiers come weak; for courtiers bring the pox into an army, and the soldiers carry it out of an army; for there is no resemblance between a courtier and a soldier, but by that disease; for the pox make courtiers and soldiers like unto like.

CAPTAIN. Well, leaving the pox to courtiers, how shall we that are soldiers, live?

LIEUTENANT. We must rob on the King's highway.

CAPTAIN. So we may chance to be hanged.

LIEUTENANT. If we be, the care of a livelihood will be at an end.

CAPTAIN. But I would not venture my life for a little money.

LIEUTENANT. How ignorantly you talk, Captain! for do not all soldiers venture their lives in battle for other men's sakes or quarrels, and have no reward for their venture and danger? and will such soldiers be afraid to venture their lives for themselves, and their lives' maintenances?

CAPTAIN. But there is hope to escape death in a battle, but there is no hope for a man to escape death when as his neck is in a noose.

LIEUTENANT. There is as little hope to escape death when as we have no means to live; and for my part, I had rather be hanged than starved; but howsoever, I am a soldier both in spirit and profession, who fears not death; and you seem to be a soldier in name, and not in nature [as] you have the title of a valiant warring man, which is a soldier, and the nature of a coward; otherwise, you would not talk of escaping death, which shows you fear death.

CAPTAIN. If you were not my approved friend, you should find I were no coward as to fear to fight with you; but I am afraid to die a base death, as a thief, and not like a soldier.

COLONEL. How strangely you talk, Captain! are not all soldiers thieves? Do not all soldiers plunder? Do not they take the spoils of the enemies? As first, kill their enemies, or take the prisoners, and then seize on their goods, and all by force? and all force is hostility, and hostility robbery; and do not only the common soldiers, but we commanders, nay, our generals do the same? and yet you name thievery and robbery base, which baseness you and many more of all degrees and qualities have practiced and lived with this dozen years to my knowledge, and it hath been a practice ever since the world began: for Adam and Eve robbed God's apple-tree, for they were forbid to take, or eat, and yet they did both; and did not Cain kill his brother Abel? and was not the Devil an enemy from the beginning? Thus robbery, malice, murder and disobedience begun from the world's creation, and will last to the world's dissolution; by which we may see, that our profession, which is to rob, fight and kill, is the most ancient profession that is.

LIEUTENANT. Dear Colonel, you have spoken most learnedly and truly.

CAPTAIN. But yet there is difference between a robber, a murderer, and a soldier; for it is honourable to kill our enemies in the open field: and it is lawful to possess the spoils.

COLONEL. Many times we kill our friends, especially in civil wars; and when we fight with foreigners, they never did us hurt, injury, or malice; but what do you talk of such honour as warring-honour, which is a fair name to a foul act; and of such martial law, as is lawless and most unjust, as to take away other men's rights? 'tis all one to call black white, or white black. But there is no such thing as law, nor no such thing as honour, but what man feigns or makes; but the truth is that which men call law and honour, is power and force: for, the strongest give law; and power makes honour as it pleases.

CAPTAIN. Your learned discourse, Colonel, shall not persuade me to rob on the highway.

LIEUTENANT. What will you do then, Captain, to get a living?

CAPTAIN. I will think of some honest way to live.

COLONEL. You had best trade, and cozen[1] your customers, that is a very honest way of living; or serve and cozen your master, or deceive your mistress, that is an honest way of living; or flatter some great lord, or lie with some old lady, that is an honest way of living: or betray, or accuse some rich man, to get a morsel of his estate for a reward, that will be an honest living: or debauch a young heir to live on his luxuries and riots, or corrupt young virgins and married wives with pimping, that will be an honest and honourable living: or be a broker for the courtiers, to help them to sell their old clothes: or a rook:[2] or be a huckster for the courtiers, to bring them suitors and petitioners for a share of their bribes, that will be an honest living: or frequent taverns and ordinaries that are customed with noble guests, and leave them to pay thy share, that will be an honourable living; and an hundred such ways there be, to get an honest living.

CAPTAIN. No, I will go to plow and cart, first.

LIEUTENANT. What? will you be a slave to a horse's tail?

COLONEL. No, no, I will tell you a better way for you, and the lieutenant, and myself to live, than that; let us get some of our poor whores that followed the army; and go into New-found Land,[3] to help to increase plantation.

CAPTAIN. Content Colonel, but let me tell you, it will be but a rotten plantation.

COLONEL. Faith all plantations are but rottenly begun; but the

---

1 cozen] To cheat, deceive, or fraud.
2 rook] A trickster, hustler.
3 New-found Land] Now a province of Canada, the region was formally claimed for England by Sir Humphrey Gilbert in 1583, and its rich fishing resources became vital to English commerce.

more rotten the planters are, the better; for rottenness doth, like as dung, help to manure the land.

LIEUTENANT.   Faith Colonel, I like your proposition so well, as I would be there.

CAPTAIN.   So do I, wherefore let us sit and provide for our journey presently, and sing this song.

THE SONG

(1)

CAPTAIN.   Let's go to our new plantation;
              Let's go to our new plantation;
              And there we do hope,
              No fear of a rope;
              Nor hanging in that blessed nation.

(2)

LIEUTENANT. Let's go to our new plantation;
            Let's go to our new plantation;
            For here's no regard,
            Nor soldier's reward,
            In this most wicked nation.

(3)

COLONEL.   Let's go to our new plantation;
              Let's go to our new plantation;
              Each man with his whore;
              Although we be poor,
              And rottenness is our foundation.

At the end of the Song, Enter Peg Valorousa.

PEG.   Then the Captain sings the burden of an old ballad.[1]

---

1   ballad] Ballet F1. "To sing the burden" of a song is to sing the chorus or refrain.

CAPTAIN.   Get thy coat Peg,
            Get thy coat Peg,
            Get thy coat Peg,
            Get thy coat Peg, and go away with me.

PEG.   You seem to be very merry brother, that your officers and you sing so cheerfully.

LIEUTENANT.   By your favour Mistress, some for joy do weep, and some for sorrow sing; witness the lamentation, and the poetical swan; and tears are often produced by laughter.

PEG.   What is the cause of your sorrowful singing?

CAPTAIN.   The army is cashiered, and so the soldiers are undone.

PEG.   It were better the soldiers should be undone, than the kingdom.

CORNET.   Will you speak against your brother's profession?

PEG.   Yes, if it be for the general peace of my native country.

CAPTAIN.   But now there is peace, how shall we live?

PEG.   You must live in peace by your wits, as you lived the wars by your valours.

LIEUTENANT.   But all the Cavalier party lost their wits when they lost their estates.

PEG.   Then you must petition the state of this kingdom to build so large a Bethlam[1] as to put in all the poor mad Cavaliers.

CAPTAIN.   Your advice is good, and you shall deliver their petition, Peg; but before I go to Bethlam I will go tell Harry Sensible and Will Fullwit the news.

LIEUTENANT.   And the Cornet and I will go drink some cordial waters to revive our spirits.

[*Exeunt*]

Enter Anne Sensible, and Jane Fullwit.

ANNE.   Do you hear the news of the cashiered army?

---

1   Bethlam] A variant spelling of "Bethlehem" or "Bedlam," a famous hospital for the mad in London.

PEG. Yes.

JANE. And are you not troubled at the news?

PEG. No; for I had rather my brother should be poor with safety, than rich with danger; but your brothers, although they have not been such active sufferers, yet they have been passive sufferers.

JANE. Yes, faith, they have had their shares of losses; but now my brother is poor, he begins to study.

PEG. What doth he study, his losses?

JANE. No, he studies books.

PEG. What books? *The Crumbs of Comfort*, and *The Sovereign Salve, for the Cure of the Soul*?[1]

JANE. All our brothers had need to study and read a cure for their estates; but let us go and bear them company.

Exeunt Anne and Jane.

Enter Mistress Prudence to Peg.

PRUDENCE. Cousin Peg, where are your companions, Nan and Jane?

PEG. They are in the chamber, envying your good fortune, and repining at their own ill fortune.

PRUDENCE. What good fortune do they envy me for?

PEG. For being the only child, and so the only heir to a rich father.

PRUDENCE. If their brothers had been as wise as my father, not to have been so vain to have showed their valour, they might have been so prudent as to have kept their estates; and so you and they would not have lost your portions by the folly of your brothers.

PEG. It was not through their folly, but through their loyalty that they entered into the action of war.

Enter Anne and Jane.

---

1   *The Crumbs...*]Fictitious titles of Christian pamphlets, akin to those published during and after the Civil War.

NAN. O Mistress Prudence! 'tis a wonder to see you abroad, or at home without a gallant.

PRUDENCE. When I come to see great beauties, such as you are, I dare not bring any of my gallants, for fear you should rob me of them.

JANE. It would be a charity to bestow some of the richest of your suitors among us poor virgins, to make husbands of; and to choose one of the poorest of our brothers to be your husband.

PRUDENCE. Indeed it would be a charity to your brothers, but no charity to myself.

Enter Master Save-all, Mistress Prudence's Father.

SAVE-ALL. Save you young beauties.

PEG. We know not whether our beauties will save us; but we shall hardly save our beauties long; for old Father Time will take them from us.

SAVE-ALL. Then you must get good and rich husbands in the time of your beauties.

PEG. There are three difficult things to get; as first, to get a husband; next, a good husband; and last, a rich husband; for men care not for handsome wives, but rich wives; for had not my cousin Prudence, your daughter, wealth as well as beauty, she might have many lovers, but not a husband amongst them all.

SAVE-ALL. Cousin Peg, you may get a rich husband, not only by means of your beauty, but by your wit.

PEG. I have heard, that in former ages, that many men did live by their wits; but in this age wit is out of fashion, and so out of practice, and so poor, as 'tis almost strange.

Enter Captain.

SAVE-ALL. I am talking to your sister my cousin Peg, and I perceive she despairs of getting a rich husband.

CAPTAIN. She hath reason, being poor herself; wherefore Peg, and her two dear friends, Mistress Anne, and Mistress Jane, must lead apes in hell.[1]

ANNE.   If the Devil hath as many apes as men follies, we shall never be able to lead them all.

SAVE-ALL.   For fear my daughter should lead apes in hell, I will go and get her a husband.

[*Exeunt*]

---

1   apes in hell] The traditional fate of old maids—see also Shakespeare's *Much Ado About Nothing* II, i, 34-41.

ACT II

SCENE I

Enter William Fullwit, and set at a Table with many Books about
him. He reads. Enter to William Fullwit, Captain and
Harry Sensible.

HARRY. Bacchus[1] and Mercury help thee, and have mercy on
thee, for I perceive you are falling into perdition, as from a
drunkard to a student; from a merry companion, to a dull
stoic; from a wit to a fool.

WILL. I pray thee Harry leave me, for I am studying to be a
wise man.

CAPTAIN. Faith Will, wisdom is not learned by the book, but
by practice, which gets experience; for wisdom lives with
living men, more than with dead authors: but prithee tell
us, what books are you reading?

WILL. I am reading Plutarch's *Lives*, Thucydides, Machiavel,
Commineus, Lucan, Caesar's *Commentaries*, and the like.[2]

HARRY. Why such books, since you are neither Greek nor
Roman? So that those histories, or historians of other
nations will not benefit thee, nor thy native country for
their laws, customs, or humours; for what are the laws, customs, humours and governments of the Romans, Greeks,
Turks, or Persians to thee, or thy native country?

CAPTAIN. You say true, Harry; and what are their wars, or
peace to us, unless the same cause, the same places, and the
same men, were again in our time? For put the case you
were General, and were to fight a battle, and would make
Caesar your pattern, it were a thousand to one but you
would show yourself rather a fool, than a Caesar; for first,
the causes of war would be different; the situation of war

---

1 Bacchus] The Greek god of wine.

2 I am rereading…] All of these are famous Greek (Plutarch, Thucydides), Roman
(Caesar, Lucan), or continental (Machiavelli, Philippe de Comines) historians,
poets, and commentators, who wrote chiefly about political issues and whose language is notoriously formal and challenging. Harry has embarked upon an overtly
ambitious course of reading.

different; the humours of the soldiers different; the habiliments,[1] postures, and breeding of the men different; the means, supplies, supports, arms, time, places and seasons different: so that if later commanders should follow the precepts of former commanders and old warriors, they would be losers; and instead of being famed good soldiers, get the reproach of being ill conductors.

HARRY. You say right, Captain; and as for foreign government, history is of no use, unless you would bring an innovation; for which, had you the power to make combustions,[2] you would sooner ruin the kingdom, than alter the government; besides, in all alterations, Fortune hath greater power, and is more predominant than prudence: wherefore leave thy impertinent studies.

WILL. I will take your counsel.

Enter Lieutenant drunk, and comes reeling in.

LIEUTENANT. Captain——Captain—— I would fain speak, very—— fain speak a speech—— but I shall be out of my speech, before I begin, and that would be a very foul disgrace—— to a man of parts.

CAPTAIN. 'Tis true, Lieutenant; but a drunken man hath no parts, for he is a departed man, Lieutenant.

LIEUTENANT. But I would have declared the strange effects ——the magical effects——the mystical effects——and the tyrannical effects.

CAPTAIN. All which effects meet in one effect, which is to be drunk, Lieutenant.

LIEUTENANT. That is true Captain—— but the strange postures, several humours, senseless brains, and disabled limbs—— is that which I would declare.

WILL. They will declare themselves, Lieutenant, without the help of rhetoric.

---

1   habilements] Equipment, array, attire.
2   combustions] "Violent excitement or commotion, disorder, confusion, tumult, hubbub (exceedingly common in 17th and 18th c.)" (*OED*).

LIEUTENANT.   You are a fool, Will; for they will want help, as you may perceive by me—— up——

He reels as he speaks.

WILL.   But words are too weak to support them.
LIEUTENANT.   But words may excuse them.

Enter Mistress Peg.

PEG.   Brother, there is a gentlewoman without, that came with the lieutenant, who says she will not go without him.
CAPTAIN.   Lieutenant, there is a gentlewoman stays to support thee to thy rest.
LIEUTENANT.   It is a cousin of mine—newly come out of the country[1]— but I will go to her—up—
CAPTAIN.   We will help to lead thee to her.

They lead him forth.

Exeunt Men.

Enter Mistress Jane, and Mistress Anne, to Mistress Peg.

JANE.   Where is the Lieutenant? 'tis said, he is so drunk, he can neither stand nor speak.
PEG.   The truth is, he doth both, but ill-favouredly.

Enter Mistress Informer.

PEG.   Mistress Informer, you are welcome.
INFORMER.   I know that, otherwise I would not visit you; but I seldom fail seeing you once a day, unless I be out of town; but now I came out of charity, knowing you were all alone.

---

1   a cousin … in the country] Possibly an allusion to the flood of people coming in to London after the Restoration; also, country women were proverbially naïve and likely to be exploited sexually by worldly courtiers. William Wycherley's *The Country Wife* (1675) revolves around this notion.

PEG.   How did you know we were all alone?

INFORMER.   Because I met your brother, Captain Valour, and Harry Sensible, Mistress Anne's brother, going up the street.

JANE.   Was not my brother with them?

INFORMER.   No; I saw Will Fullwit go to the play-house.

JANE.   What play-house? the gaming-house, or the acting-house?[1]

INFORMER.   The acting-house.

ANNE.   Our brothers might be so kind, as sometimes to carry us to plays.

PEG.   So they would, if we were such cousins as the Lieutenant had here; but being their sisters, they will not be troubled with us.

INFORMER.   Now you talk of the Lieutenant, it puts me in mind, I met him in the street leading a gentlewoman.

PEG.   I believe she rather led him, than he her.

INFORMER.   I know not which, led which; but neither of them did walk steadily, for sometimes they went towards the wall, and then presently towards the kennel.[2]

PEG.   It was a sign they were both drunk. But Mistress Informer, have you brought the new-fashioned hankerchief to see.

INFORMER.   Yes, but I have left it in your chamber.

PEG.   Come let us go see it.

Exeunt all but Jane.

Enter Will Fullwit muffled in his Cloak.

WILL.   Sister Jane, is Harry Sensible within?

JANE.   I cannot tell whether he be returned; but he was abroad.[3]

WILL.   Pray see; and if he be returned, bid him come to me.

---

1   What play house?] "To play" means both "to gamble" and "to act in a play."
2   kennel] "The surface drain of a street, the gutter" (*OED*).
3   abroad.] abroad? F1

Enter Harry Sensible, Will Fullwit upon the ground, he groans,
Harry Sensible runs and embraces him.

HARRY.   Dear Will, what is the cause you lie so sadly?

WILL.   Oh, oh, I am wounded, wounded.

HARRY.   Where? where? Tell me dear Will.

WILL.   I am killed, I am killed.

HARRY.   By whom?

WILL.   I die, I die.

HARRY.   Hold life a little time, so long to tell thine enemy, that
I may sacrifice him on the tomb; Oh he is dead: dear Will,
I wish to die, since thou art gone.

Exit Harry Sensible weeping.

After he was gone out, Will Fullwit rises and dances,—then enter
Harry Sensible, with Captain Valour, Lieutenant Fightwell, and
Cornet Defendant, all stand as in amaze.

CAPTAIN.   Harry, did not you tell us, that Will Fullwit was
killed?

HARRY.   I thought him dead.

CAPTAIN.   Then how the Devil comes he to be alive again?

Enter Mistress Anne Sensible as in haste.

ANNE.   O, where is Mr. Fullwit's body?

He addresses to her.

WILL.   Dear lady, I, for thy dear sake,
Will travel to the Stygian lake;[1]
There let us meet, and then embrace,
And look each other in the face.

---

1   Stygian lake]The river Styx, that surrounds the infernal regions in Greek mythology.

ANNE. O the Lord, what doth he ail?

Enter Mistress Peg Valourosa.

WILL. O stand away,
For there breaks day;
The sun doth rise,
Dazzling mine eyes:
For you the goddess are of light,
She's a fiend that governs night.

HARRY. By heaven he is stark mad.

Will Fullwit draws his sword.

WILL. Here I will fight
As champion knight.

The Ladies run squealing away.

WILL. What, are they gone?
They do me wrong.

LIEUTENANT. You have frightened them away.

HARRY. Dear Will, put up thy sword, for we are all thy friends.

WILL. You are my foes, I say,
Wherefore away.

HARRY. This madness is worse, far worse than death.

Harry Sensible weeps.

WILL. What Harry, do you weep in earnest?

HARRY. How can I choose, to see my friend in a mad distemper?

WILL. Why Harry, I have only acted an intrigue.

CAPTAIN. A pox of your intrigue; for you have frightened the ladies, and disturbed your friends.

LIEUTENANT. Nay faith, he hath disturbed the ladies, and frightened his friends.

HARRY. But how came you to be in this humour?

WILL. With seeing a new play.

CORNET. But you have not acted an intrigue yet.

WILL. That's true, by reason the ladies went away, and Harry's tears would not suffer me to make more changes; besides I had not time to express, or act my intrigue; but if you will call the ladies again, you shall see me act an intrigue and catastrophe, as it ought to be.

HARRY. Hang intrigues and catastrophes, and play the fool no more.

CAPTAIN. Prithee Will, go with us to a tavern, and there we will have several sorts of wine, changes of music, and variety of mistresses, which are better intrigues and catastrophes than are acted upon the stage.

WILL. Content, let us go, to dry up Harry's rheum with sack, and to let him see I am still a merry companion.

HARRY. If I had known you had dissembled, I would not have discovered my love.

WILL. Why? Love and deceit is an intrigue; but the truth is, I did this, that you and the Captain should not believe that I was a dull stoic.

Enter Dick Traveller, as newly returned home.

WILL. Dick Traveller, art thou returned, old blade, from thy foreign travels, to thy home-friends?

DICK. I confess foreign travellers are apt to lose home-friends.

WILL. But you have not lost us, for thou art heartily welcome.

HARRY. 'Tis a sign that your travels have been as cold as far, for you have brought white hairs home with you.

LIEUTENANT. He could not avoid a white head; for he hath been at the north pole, which hath turned his hairs to snow.

DICK. I have been near the pole in Greenland.

CORNET. Is that country fertile?

DICK. Yes, of frost and snow.

CORNET. Is it populous?

DICK. 'Tis very populous of bears and foxes.

LIEUTENANT. Is it a good place for plantation?

DICK. Yes faith, for if there were a colony of adulterers sent thither, they might plant chastity; and if a colony of drunkards were sent thither, they might plant temperance; also if a colony of prodigals were sent thither, they might plant frugality.

WILL. But might not a colony of fools plant wit there?

LIEUTENANT. It were excellent policy, to send all the fools thither.

DICK. Those parts of the world would not hold them, if all be sent; for most men are fools.

CAPTAIN. Why fools in what part of the world soever, they live in twilight; and near the pole is twilight half the year.

WILL. Prithee let's leave talking of such cold elements; for the very hearing of the north pole hath chilled my spirits, as if they were hard frozen, and all my thoughts are turned to snow; wherefore let's go to a tavern, and drink sack to thaw them.

DICK. I shall bear you company.

WILL. Faith thou hast reason to drink ten fathom deep to melt thy frozen body, and thaw thy cold blood that is turned to ice, and spirits of life may swim in full large veins.

DICK. You are full of poetical fancy.

WILL. 'Tis a sign I did never travel to the north pole, for fancy lies in east and western brains; the truth is, every poet's brain is a torrid zone; wherefore let's go to the tavern.

HARRY. That is under the ecliptic line.

Enter Peg and Anne.

CAPTAIN. Are you come to see the intrigue?

PEG. No, but we are come to see, whether Will Fullwit be not dead again.

WILL. No; but I am not so well, but that these good fellows, are going to give me a cordial.

DICK. To me these ladies are cordials.

WILL.   You have not tasted them yet.

DICK.   May I presume to salute[1] you, ladies?

He salutes them.

HARRY.   How do you like them?

DICK.   It is not a question to be asked, nor I to give an answer.

CAPTAIN.   Prithee come away, and leave complimenting.

Enter Jane. Exeunt Men.

PEG.   Did you see Dick Traveller.

JANE.   Yes, I met him, and all the crew of them.

PEG.   I have seen thy brother stark mad.

JANE.   I never knew him otherwise.

ANNE.   He did only show an intrigue.

Enter Mistress Informer.

PEG.   Mistress Informer, you are welcome; but what news brought you hither?

INFORMER.   Hearing Master Traveller was to see you.

PEG.   He was so.

INFORMER.   Pray what new fashions hath he brought from the north pole?

PEG.   I do not perceive any new fashion.

INFORMER.   Lord, how reports prove false! for I heard he had a strange fashioned suit of clothes which he did wear, made all of ice, and a great thick cap of snow, which he wore over his head; and that the motions of his body and behaviour were trembling and shaking, as if he were affrighted, or in a cold fit of an ague, and that his language was such a stuttering and stammering language, as not any man in these parts could understand him.

---

1   a salute] A kiss was the common form of greeting between men and women in the 17th century.

PEG. I saw no such clothes or cap that he wore, nor heard no such stuttering, stammering language.

INFORMER. Indeed, as to his garments, I did not believe reports; for I said to those persons, that told that report for a certain truth, that I could sooner believe he was accoutered in a suit of fire, rather than of ice; but they replied, that those parts of the world, so near the poles, would not permit fire, for the extreme cold did put out all sorts of fire; but pray tell me whether he doth not look very pale, withered, dry and old.

PEG. He doth not look as if he were a very young man, because he is in some years; but he looks well for his age.

INFORMER. What kind of men, doth Mr. Traveller say are natives at the pole?

PEG. I did not hear him say, there be either native men or women.

INFORMER. If not, how did he get a mistress?

JANE. Such cold elements do not require courtship.

INFORMER. But are there not any living creatures there?

PEG. Yes, there are bears; and in some of the islands near the poles, there are white bears, with red patches on their heads.

INFORMER. That is very fine, and surely very becoming; wherefore I will inform the ladies, who I am sure will follow that fashion.

ANNE. How can they be in the bears' fashion?

INFORMER. Very easily; for they nay have a white satin gown, and a red velvet cap; and so be like the white bears, with the red patches on their heads.

PEG. If they imitate nothing else of the bear but that, it will not be much amiss.

INFORMER. Fare you well; for I long to carry the news of the fashion.

Exit.

Enter Will Fullwit.

WILL. Is Harry returned?

ANNE. No.

Exeunt Women.

Enter Harry.

WILL. I was going to the tavern, believing you and the rest of our companions, were gone to the tavern.

HARRY. I stay for Dick Traveller; but Captain Valour, Lieutenant Fightwell, and Cornet Defendant, are gone before to the tavern, to provide us good wine.

WILL. They will be drunk before we come.

HARRY. Surely they will forbear drinking until we come.

WILL. How should they forbear drinking, if they went to taste the wine?

HARRY. They went to bespeak good wine, and not to taste it.

WILL. Hang them, they will taste pint after pint, and quart after quart; for they have not so much temperance as to stay.

Enter Dick Traveller.

WILL. Dick, a pox take you for staying, for the Captain, Lieutenant, and Cornet have drank all the wine in the tavern by this time.

DICK. They cannot drink all.

WILL. Yes but they can; for they will pour in and out so fast, as I am confident they have not left so much as the drippings of the taps.

HARRY. Come, come, let us make haste to them.

WILL. Yes, when all is drunk up.

HARRY. I will warrant you there will be enough left to quench our drought.

WILL. I hate quenching of droughts; I would be like a ship, to swim in an ocean of wine.

Enter Mistress Informer.

INFORMER. Are your sisters within?

WILL. Yes.

Exeunt Men.

Enter Peg, Jane and Anne.

PEG. Mrs. Informer, what is the reason you are returned so soon?

INFORMER. The reason is, that I had forgot to tell you of the good company I was in the other day.

JANE. We heard that you were in sociable company.

INFORMER. I was so; and the company hath past their time with all the delightful recreations that could be devised, for the time they associated together; for sometimes the ladies, and their courting servants, played cards, and sometimes danced, and sometimes feasted, and some of the fairest ladies sat to have their pictures drawn, whilst their lovers or friends gazed on their faces; which was an occasion to cause those ladies to put their faces into their best countenances; and some of the gallants did make their mistresses' portraitures, both in verse and prose, whilst the painter did draw their pictures in oil or watercolours.

PEG. It seems the gallants were courtly to the ladies.

INFORMER. They were so.

JANE. Do the men court the women publicly or *incognito*?

INFORMER. They court both ways; for every man hath, his particular, which he doth usher; but if they like each other's lady and mistress better than their own, or love's variety, or would be liked, or loved by more than his own woman: they make love *incognito*, as in a mystical or allegorical way; which allegorical-love's making, or wooing, pleases the women infinitely, as by [side] eye-glances, languishing looks, smothered sighs, and metaphorical speeches; as also wrying their necks,[1] with their eyes fixed on the ground, or falling, or stumbling upon them, as if it were by chance;

---

1 wrying their necks] Averting their faces by twisting their necks.

and many the like behaviours, garbs, motions, countenances and discourses; as I cannot remember to repeat all; and some are so excellent and well experienced in the art of making love *incognito* allegorically, or metaphorically, as I have known or observed one man to make half a dozen women at least at one time, believe he hath been deeply in love with each of them.

JANE. And do the women receive these fashioned courtships in the like manner?

INFORMER. Yes, for they are as expert as the men in those ways; the truth is, that although every man and every woman hath a staple servant, and a staple mistress, yet they traffic all in common.

JANE. It seems they are common wooers: but farewell, I must go speak with my brother Fullwit.

INFORMER. You must go to the tavern then.

JANE. Why, is he gone to the tavern?

INFORMER. Yes, I did hear him, Mr. Sensible, and Mr. Traveller say, they would go unto the Crown Tavern.

PEG. I am sure my brother and his officer are there before them.

JANE. It is not to be endured they should spend so much, and we want so much as we do.

INFORMER. If I might advise you ladies, I would have you go and bear them company.

JANE. We will take your advice, although not to drink, yet to quarrel, and you shall be our conductor.

PEG. Those that see us will believe that Mrs. Informer is a bawd, that conducts three young wenches to some gentlemen in the tavern.

INFORMER. Come, come, for if I be, it is not the first time I have been taken for a bawd.

Exeunt.

SCENE II

*Enter Captain Valour, Lieutenant Fightwell, and Cornet Defendant,
as in a tavern, who drink whilst they talk.*

CORNET. Captain, let us not stay for, Harry Will and Dick, but drink in the meantime.

CAPTAIN. Content, let us sit close, and drink hard; for here is the best wine; it was drawn out of Bacchus' cellar, wherefore it is divine wine.

LIEUTENANT. If it be divine, we should pray before we drink.

CAPTAIN. No you must drink first, as into a drunken humour with divine wine, and then pray when the spirit is strong in you.

LIEUTENANT. It is unnatural, Captain, at least for martial men to pray; in so much, that if a soldier should be seen or heard to pray, he would be thought a coward.

CAPTAIN. That is not so, for we were beaten by those that prayed.

CORNET. But some of our party prayed.

CAPTAIN. If they did, it was so softly, as Jupiter could not hear them: but I have drunk myself into a loving humour, I wish I had a wench.

CORNET. We will knock for the chamberlain.

Enter Chamberlain.

CAPTAIN. Chamberlain, get us some wenches.

CHAMBERLAIN. There are none to be had, sir.

CAPTAIN. You are a lying rogue; for there hath been no age, nor there is not a kingdom that is not fully stored with them.

CHAMBERLAIN. There is store in the kingdom, if it please your worship, but they are not for soldiers in this age.

CAPTAIN. You lie, you rogue, they are for the soldiers in all ages, even in the worst of times; for they will venture their lives to follow the army for the pleasure of a soldier.

CHAMBERLAIN. An't please your worship, it is for the hopes of gaining some of the soldier's plunder; but now that your worships can neither get plunder nor pay, they defy you, and will not come near you, but laugh at you, and say you are like old rusty arms out of fashion, and that they are now for the court, not the camp.

[*Exit*]

CAPTAIN. Damned Fortune, shall the court rob us, both of wealth and pleasure?

*Enter Will Fullwit, Harry Sensible,
and Dick Traveller, the Captain drinking
when they came in.*

WILL. Hold, hold, Captain, what a devil, are you mad to drink before we come?
CAPTAIN. You are mad to stay so long, would you have us choked for thrift?
DICK. Come, come, we shall overtake them.
CAPTAIN. But you shall not, for we will, now you are come, sit and drink healths, as health for health.
WILL. Is there wine enough to drink healths?
CAPTAIN. Enough, Will, enough.

They sit down and call for wine.

CAPTAIN. Dick, you are not returned as a traveler *à la mode*.
DICK. Would you have me *à la mode* de bear, or *à la mode* de fox.
CAPTAIN. Why not as well as other travelers, that return *à la mode* de ape, and *à la mode* de ass?
WILL. Well, leaving the bears, foxes, asses and apes; here is a health to the North Star.
HARRY. That is a very cold star, Will.

WILL.   Therefore I will drink the health in sack, to heat it into a sun.

HARRY.   And I will drink a health to Virtue.

CAPTAIN.   You had better put ice into your wine than Virtue; for she is so cold, not any heat can thaw her; but I will drink a health more proper, for Dick Traveller's company, which are the seven deadly sins.

DICK.   They belong more to the courtier than the traveler; yet I will pledge them, were they seventy seven sins, and drink them all at a draught.

LIEUTENANT.   But that is unconscionable to drink them all, leaving not any for your friends.

DICK.   All those I account my friends, that have wit enough to get, or invent more; for new-fashioned sins are as easily devised as new-fashioned garments.

WILL.   Who is the maker of new-fashioned sins?

DICK.   The Devil.

Enter Jane, Anne, Peg, and Informer.

CAPTAIN.   But what the devil makes these women come hither?

WILL.   Ladies, this is boldly done, to come and drink healths with us.

CAPTAIN.   'Tis but changing of sisters, and they will serve us for wenches, and Mrs. Informer, my Cornet or Lieutenant shall pay her for their company.

JANE.   We came not to drink, but to complain that our brothers should be so unkind, unworthy and unnatural, to sit drinking to fill their heads, and empty their purses, when we want meat and clothes.

PEG.   You can be jovial, but we must be melancholy; you sing catches, when we shed tears.

ANNE.   You have many bottles of wine, when we want smocks to our backs.

WILL.   But you have silk gowns.

JANE.   Yes, such as you buy at the second hand, or at some

broker's shop, which are more rotten than the Jews' clothes in the wilderness.[1]

HARRY. Why, what would you have us to do?

ANNE. Not to sit, drinking in a tavern most of your time; but to seek and endeavour to get some good offices and employments that may help to repair your ruins, and to maintain us according to our births and breedings.

WILL. Faith, we may seek, and not find; beg, and not get.

PEG. But yet you shall not need to spend that little which is left in drink.

LIEUTENANT. If it were not for drink, we should run mad; but drink drowns all sorts of sorrows.

CAPTAIN. Leave your caterwauling, and get you hence.

PEG. We will not go home, unless you will go with us.

WILL. Yes, so it will be thought, you are our wenches, not known you are our sisters.

JANE. We care not what people think, knowing ourselves honest.

HARRY. Come, let us go, otherwise they will scold so loud, as all the street will be in a hubbub to know the cause.

Exeunt.

SCENE III

Enter Father [Save-all] and his Daughter [Prudence].

SAVE-ALL. Daughter, you are being now marriageable, I am resolved to provide you a good husband.

PRUDENCE. I am willing to be a wife; but pray pardon me if I ask you what you mean by a good husband?

SAVE-ALL. A good husband, is a prudent husband.

PRUDENCE. That is a miserable and jealous husband.

---

1 Jew's clothes in the wilderness] A reference to the biblical book of Exodus, in which Moses led his people out of Egypt and into the desert for "four hundred and thirty years" (Exodus 12:40).

SAVE-ALL. No, no, mistake me not, for miserableness and jealousy are extremes, but prudence is a mean.

PRUDENCE. If I must marry according to a moral mean, which is between extremes, then I must marry a man of a mean birth, mean breeding, mean estate, mean wit, mean judgment, mean understanding, mean esteem, mean behaviour, and the like.

SAVE-ALL. No daughter, I only desire you not to be an extreme fool, as to marry to extreme misery; but since you dispute for wisdom or discretion, I'll give you leave to make your own choice, which will tend either to my grief or comfort; to your own happiness or unhappiness; and I shall see whether you can act as wisely, as you plead wittily.

Exit Save-all, and then enters a Suitor.[1]

SUITOR. Madam, your beauty is the gaze or blaze to all the world; nay, 'tis not only a mortal but an immortal light, and as the soul, not one humane creature but of all the world; which immortal light and soul I am very desirous to enjoy, and to make you my wife.

PRUDENCE. Sir, I shall readily consent, upon condition you make me a present of the Alkabest, and a jointure of the Elixir.[2]

Exit Prudence, Suitor solus.

SUITOR. This lady is not to be won with compliments of learning.

Enter another gentleman.

---

1 s.d.] This stage direction is immediately followed by another ("Enter the young lady, and a young gentleman a suitor to her"), which I have omitted for clarity.
2 Alkabest ... Elixir] Equipment and terms used in alchemy, suitable for defusing the suitor's mystical terms of adoration.

GENTLEMAN.   Well met sir; have you seen the lady?

SUITOR.   Yes.

GENTLEMAN.   And how do you agree?

SUITOR.   Just as chemists and fire.

GENTLEMAN.   How is that?

SUITOR.   That is, they do not agree at all, but delude and cross each other.

GENTLEMAN.   Nay, faith, if she be in a cross humour, I will not plead and present my suit to her today.

[Exeunt]

SCENE IV

Enter Harry, and walks in a musing posture.

Enter Captain.

CAPTAIN.   What is the cause you walk in such a musing posture Harry?

HARRY.   I have lost my mistress.

CAPTAIN.   Is that all?

HARRY.   Yes, and too much.

CAPTAIN.   Art thou mad?

HARRY.   No.

CAPTAIN.   Have you any wit?

HARRY.   Why do you ask?

CAPTAIN.   Because you are melancholy for a woman.

HARRY.   It would make you or any man melancholy, to lose such a woman as my mistress is.

CAPTAIN.   Faith, not unless my mistress were the only woman in the world.

HARRY.   She was the only woman in my affection.

CAPTAIN.   'Tis a sign thy affection is a poor, mean, low, narrow, and little affection, that hath but one room for one mistress; whereas, my affection is as large as the Grand Signior's seraglio,—— for it will hold hundreds of mistresses, with all their maids and slaves attending upon them; the truth is, my affection will hold all the women in the world; for I love all women-kind, in so much as I can never want love so long as there be women, or a woman; and surely I can never want a woman so long as the world doth last; for the world doth not increase anything so numerously as women; for all armies, nations, cities, towns, villages, houses, churches and chambers are for the most part filled with women; and since there are so many women, it were a madness for to be melancholy for the loss of one woman: wherefore put off this whining humour for shame, and get another mistress; and if I might advise you, I would have four and twenty mistresses, at least, at one time, and so you will have a mistress for every hour of the day and night.

HARRY.   But my mistress is a woman that doth excel all her sex.

CAPTAIN.   In what?

HARRY.   In beauty, wit and virtue.

CAPTAIN.   Nay, if you talk of virtue in a mistress, you are mad indeed.

HARRY.   May not a man have a virtuous mistress?

CAPTAIN.   No, for it is against the rules and nature of virtue, to live in a mistress; for virtue is an humble servant, when as a mistress is an imperious tyrant; for women are insolent and imperious so long as they are made mistresses, which is to be flattered, attended and served with men's estates, bodies and souls; but when they come to be wives, which is to be slaves, perchance, they may have so much of virtue, as to be somewhat humble, when as they are forced to serve, and cannot command; but a wise man will never have a mistress, although he should live unmarried, but he will keep a maidservant for his use, and so take and turn away so often as he pleases: but is thy mistress dead?

HARRY.   No but she is married.

CAPTAIN.   Why then, she may be her husband's servant, and thy mistress still?

HARRY.   But she is too virtuous to be my mistress now she is another man's wife.

CAPTAIN. I prithee be not so wedded to the opinion of women's virtues; for that will hinder thee from pursuing a lover's design.

HARRY. I will endeavour to forget this mistress. And get another.

CAPTAIN. Now you speak like a wise man.

Enter Will to the Captain and Harry.

WILL. Captain, and Harry, I was even now wishing for either of you.

HARRY. If you be as fortunate in all your wishes, as in either of our being here, you will be the most fortunate and happiest man that ever was; but tell us whether it was your affection, appetite or reason, which was the cause of your wish.

WILL. Not any of them; for it was my wit that caused that wish; for I have made a copy of verses, which I would have you both read, and then give me your opinion.

CAPTAIN. For my part, I had rather your appetite had wished for our good fellowship; for I had rather drink a health, than read a copy of verses; the truth is, I cannot endure verses.

WILL. But if they were a copy made in your mistress's praise you would like them.

CAPTAIN. I should hate my mistress, through the hate to the verses, were she never so worthy. Or the verses so witty.

WILL. That makes thee love mean common women.

CAPTAIN. They are fools that will woo a nice lady with flattering verses, when they may have a free wench, with plain prose; and as the old saying, Joan in the dark is as good as my lady.[1]

HARRY. Nay faith, but they are not; for all common wenches are unwholesome sluts.

WILL. Well, leaving Joan and a lady at this present, I would have you read a drunken song, which I made to sing between every glass, for singing dries the throat, and

---

1 Joan in...] Proverbial in the seventeenth century.

drought requires drink, all which will make us drink with more gust,[1] and the wine will taste the quicker.

CAPTAIN. Faith, I hate verse so much, as the song will make me vomit up my drink, besides singing brings down rheum, and to have salt rheum mixed with sharp wine, will cause such an unpleasing taste, which will make us more sick than Grocus Mettallorum,[2] and spoil the wine; wherefore burn your song; besides, let me tell you, as your friend, that 'tis very dangerous for a drunkard to be a poet; for the vapour of wit, and the vapour of wine, joined together, will overpower your brain, and may make a man so mad, as to be past recovery; but when the brain is only muddled with the vapour of drink, sleep cures it, and drink causes sleep; whereas poetry banishes sleep from the senses, and heats the brain into a fever.

WILL. But the hotter the brain is, the quicker the wit is, and poets drink wine to heighten their fancy.

CAPTAIN. Let me tell you, poets drink wine to please their palates; and it is an old saying, that when drink is in, then wit is out; wherefore burn thy verses.

HARRY. Do, Will take his counsel, and burn them.

WILL. I will follow your advice, and burn them to light a pipe of tobacco.

CAPTAIN. That is worse than if you should read them, or sing them; for you will suck them back into your brain, with the smoke, through your pipe, and so have your verses to return smoking hot, which will either smother your brain, or give your brain such an appetite, as you will never leave versifying. But come let us go and consult how they may be destroyed.

WILL. Content.

---

1 gust] "The individual faculty of taste" (OED).

2 Grocus Metallorum] A misspelling of Crocus Metallorum, an oxide of antimony, used as an emetic by Renaissance physicians. In *The English Physitian* (1652, popularly known as "Culpeper's *Herball*"), Nicholas Culpeper (1616-1654) includes a recipe that mixes wine with crocus metallorum and other ingredients: such a mixture would indeed "spoil the wine" with an unpleasant flavour and nasty side-effects. I am most grateful to Dr. Stephen Clucas of Birkbeck College, London, for his explanation of this term.

Enter Peg.

CAPTAIN.   Peg, have a care, and stay at home.

[*Exit Men*]

Enter Mrs. Jane Fullwit, Mrs. Anne Sensible, to Mrs. Peg Valorosa,
who walked in a melancholy posture.

ANNE.   Always melancholy?

PEG.   Who can be merry, that is poor?

JANE.   Who lives more merry than beggars?

PEG.   But our birth and breeding will not suffer us to beg.

JANE.   No, but we may live by our wits.

PEG.   But wit was killed in the war.

ANNE.   You are mistaken, it was only banished with the cavaliers; but now it is returned home.

PEG.   I cannot perceive it; for though I see many fools, yet not
a true natural wit amongst them; for there is the rhyming-
fools, the intrigue-fools, and the fine-languaged fools.

JANE.   The truth is, the multitude of fools obscure the wits,
like dark clouds that obscure the sun; but let us endeavour
to shine through those clouds.

PEG.   That cannot be.

JANE.   Let us try for our profit.

PEG.   But word-wit will not make us rich.

JANE.   I grant it, but deed-wit will do us good, wherefore let
us endeavour to get rich husbands.

PEG.   We may endeavour it, but not obtain it.

ANNE.   But if we could get them by our ingenuity, we know
not where they are to be had.

JANE.   Madam Informer will give us intelligence.

Enter Harry.

HARRY.   Is your brother within the house?

JANE.   I think he is, I will go and see.

Exeunt Women.

Enter Will Fullwit.

HARRY. Well, I shall never trust any man more for your sake, nor never believe in friendship.

WILL. Why?

HARRY. Do you ask why, when you who I did believe was so true a friend, would never forsake me at a time of need, when not only my life, but my honour was engaged in a quarrel, for which I chose you as my second, and then to fail me at the appointed time, was base; for had you been my enemy, your honour should have brought you into the field.

WILL. Faith, I was so engaged in a company of ladies, I could not come.

HARRY. Can there be a greater engagement than friendship, honour and honesty?

WILL. Can there be a greater friendship than the love of women, or more honourable than to serve the female sex? and as for honesty, 'tis not worth anything, besides, it is a fool, it brings a man to ruin, at least a man can never thrive by it.

HARRY. O judgment, how hath it erred, to choose a knave for a friend, a coward for a second!

WILL. So I perceive, rather than you will want an enemy, you will quarrel with your own judgment, you had best fight a duel with that.

HARRY. Go, go, and kiss a mistress, and leave talking of duels.

WILL. Aye marry, this is friendly advice; for in kisses there is life and pleasure, in duels death and danger; but let me tell thee, Harry, I have done thee a more friendly part, in not appearing, than ever I did thee in my life; for I have saved thy life, at least thy estate, and have kept thy honour pure and free from stains, and I have increased thy honour.

HARRY. Which way?

WILL. Thus; I have let thee go into the field for thy honour, and have kept thine enemy out, not by force, but by persuasion; which persuasion hath so wrought on him and his second, as they will both meet in the same place you quarreled in, where shall be the same company that drank, and was drunk there, and before thy company he will confess his fault, and ask pardon, which is as much satisfaction as an honest or honourable man can desire; and it would be against the laws of good fellowship to fight a sober duel, for a drunken quarrel; wherefore agree, and be friends with our drunken comrade.

Enter Captain, Cornet, Lieutenant, and Dick Traveller.

CAPTAIN.   We heard you very high in words, I hope you two dear friends will not quarrel?

WILL.   We shall not quarrel like enemies; but Harry is angry, because I will not let him fight.

CAPTAIN.   Fight, with whom will he fight?

WILL.   With Tom Ranter.

LIEUTENANT.   Hang him, he will get no honour with fighting with him.

CAPTAIN.   Come, come, I will conduct you to a better pastime than fighting vain duels; for there are a company of ladies which I am acquainted with that have made a merry meeting, only they want men to keep them company.

WILL.   Let us go; come Harry, will you go?

HARRY.   Yes, with all my heart.

Enter Peg.

CAPTAIN.   I will but speak a word to my sister.

He whispers. Exeunt Men.

Peg stands as if she were musing.

Enter Jane and Anne.

ANNE. What are you thinking of now?

PEG. I was reasoning with myself, why those women that were neither factious, ambitious, covetous, malicious nor cruel, should suffer in the wars with the men.

JANE. The gods would not be just, if the women did not suffer for the crimes of the men, since all men suffer for a single crime of a particular woman, witness our grandmother Eve.

Enter Madam Informer.

ANNE. O Madam Informer, have you made an inquiry?

INFORMER. Yes, marry have I, and find the mass of wealth is in the possession of usurers, lawyers and physicians.

JANE. I believe usurers and lawyers may be very rich, for the Civil War hath made those sorts of men like as vultures, after a battle, that feed on the dead, or dying corpse; but I cannot perceive why physicians should be the richer for those times.

INFORMER. There is great reason why they should gain the more; for both men and women's bodies are corrupted, and weakened with melancholy, grief, malice, revenge, envy, wrong, injustice, and the like; so that their bodies are full of the scurvy, which their misfortunes hath bred.

PEG. But have you found amongst these rich sorts of men, any widowers, or bachelors?

INFORMER. Yes, that I have, three bachelors; the richest amongst them, is one Mr. Get-all an usurer; the other Sergeant Plead-all a lawyer; the third Doctor Cure-all a physician.

JANE. Which is the richest?

INFORMER. The usurer; for he is worth two hundred thousand pounds.

PEG. Well, we will employ our wits to get these men.

INFORMER. But wit without assistance, will do no good; wherefore you must get your brothers, and their friends to help you by their industry.

JANE. Your counsel is good.

Exeunt,—
only Peg meets her Brother, Captain, as coming in.

PEG.   Brother, are you well, you look so melancholy?
CAPTAIN.   In body, but not in mind, Peg.

Exit Peg.

Enter Will and Harry, the Captain, and the rest.

HARRY.   Captain, what make thee so sad?
CAPTAIN.   That which would make any man sad, want of money.
WILL.   We may be as sad as you for that; but to be poor and melancholy is a double misery.
CAPTAIN.   Life cannot be merry, when it hath not anything to live upon.

Enter Dick Traveller.

CAPTAIN.   Dick, where have you been?
DICK.   I have been peeping through a key-hole into a room, where your three sisters are in serious counsel with Madam Informer.
CAPTAIN.   Pray God she is not instructing them to be wenches.
WILL.   Faith, I fear it; for she would make an ingenuous bawd.
CAPTAIN.   I will go and part them.
DICK.   Pray do not; for perchance the women's wits may do you more service than your own; for I heard them say, their brothers must assist them; and surely they do not believe you would be their pimps.
HARRY.   No, for they know we shall rather be their murderers than their pimps.
DICK.   Then let them alone; and whilst they are in a council, let us go to a tavern and drink.
CAPTAIN.   But we have no money.

DICK. I have a little credit to run on the score.

HARRY. Faith, if we go to the tavern, the girls will come crying after us.

DICK. I tell you they are so busy about some female design, as they will not miss us.

Exeunt all but the Cornet.

CORNET. I must stay to tell a lie, because they shall not follow us.

Enter Peg, Jane, and Anne.

CORNET. Ladies, your brothers bid me tell you, they are gone about some serious business; but they will return soon.

PEG. When they will.

Exit Cornet.

Enter Informer.

PEG. Mrs. Informer, how shall we three agree in the choice of the three rich men?

INFORMER. You must draw lots, and I have made them ready.

JANE. I pray Jupiter, I may draw the rich man.

ANNE. I pray Jupiter, I may draw him.

PEG. We must take our lot, let it be what it will.

Jane draws first. They draw.

INFORMER. Which have you drawn?

JANE. I have drawn Sergeant Plead-all.

Anne Sensible draws.

ANNE. I have drawn Doctor Cure-all.

PEG. Jove, I thank thee in giving the usurer to me.

INFORMER. Now go to your brothers, and inform them of your designs.

JANE. Faith, they will rather laugh at us, than help us.

ANNE. But yet we dare not do any such thing without their knowledge.

PEG. I am confident my brother will assist me.

JANE. Come, let us go to them.

Exeunt.

SCENE V

*Enter Captain, Harry, Will, Dick, Lieutenant and Cornet;
as in the Tavern.*

WILL. Well, this wine is so fresh and full of spirit, as it would make a fool a poet.

HARRY. Or a poet a fool.

DICK. Then here's a health to the most fools in the world.

CAPTAIN. Then you must drink a health to the whole world, that is one great fool.

LIEUTENANT. Prithee Dick do not drink that health, for it will choke thee; for the world of fools is too big for one draught.

DICK. Then here's a health to the wisest man.

CORNET. You may as well drink a health to a drop of water in the ocean.

CAPTAIN. Faith Dick, that health is so little, it cannot be tasted; besides, I do not love droppings.

DICK. Then here's a health to the honestest man in the world.

WILL. That health is more difficult than the last? for it is rare to know an honest man, as to see a phoenix.

DICK. Then I will drink a health to the chastest woman.

LIEUTENANT. You might as well drink a health to the queen of the fairies, which is an old wives' tale; for chastity lives only in the name not in nature.

DICK. Then here's a health to a common courtesan.

HARRY.   A pox of that health, I will not pledge it.

WILL.   Then here's a health to the Muses.

CAPTAIN.   It is a shame for a soldier to drink a health to the Muses.

LIEUTENANT.   The truth is, I hate a poetical soldier.

HARRY.   Is it not lawful for a soldier (Captain) to have wit?

CAPTAIN.   No; for wit makes the minds of men soft, sweet, gentle, and effeminate; insomuch as those that have wit, are not fit for soldiers; for soldiers should have resolute minds, cloudy thoughts, hard hearts, rough speeches, and boisterous actions.

CORNET.   The truth is (Captain) there is much difference between a poet and a soldier (which is wit and courage) as between a calm and a storm.

CAPTAIN.   You say true, Cornet; for certainly the best soldiers are born and bred in the uncivilest nations.

LIEUTENANT.   No doubt of it, Captain.

DICK.   Then here's a health to the Graces.

CAPTAIN.   That health is three times worse than the former, which was nine times too bad; for when did you know a soldier to have grace?

LIEUTENANT.   The truth is (Captain) it is unnatural for a soldier to have grace.

CAPTAIN.   You say true, Lieutenant.

WILL.   Setting aside, the Muses and the Graces, here is a health to the Furies.[1]

CAPTAIN.   I marry sir, that health sounds like a soldier's health, and I will pledge it were the glass full of wounds. Here Harry, here's the Furies' health.

HARRY.   Faith, Captain, we shall be furiously drunk with the Furies' health.

CORNET.   It will give fire to your brain.

---

1   Furies] In Greek mythology, the three female followers of Bacchus (god of wine), known for riotous and often violent behaviour. When Orestes was acquitted of the murder of his mother Clytemnestra by an Athenian jury, the Furies pursued Orestes relentlessly in a quest for revenge. Only when Athena promised them a sanctuary in Athens dedicated to them did they cease their pursuit; henceforth they were known as the Eumenides, or "kindly ones," a radical transformation of their original nature.

HARRY. Yes, and burn out my reason.

They drink.

CAPTAIN. Now I will begin another health; here gentlemen, here is Death's health.

DICK. Good Captain, do not drink Death's health, for it will make our wine so cold it will never warm us; besides, dead wine will never make us drunk; and if we had not a desire to be drunk, we should not have come to now the tavern.

CAPTAIN. Dick, you must drink Death's health, for Death's health will make you dead drunk.

DICK. Then I will drink it, and invite you and the rest of the society to my funeral.

CAPTAIN. Then we will carry thee to thy bed with ceremony, as to thy grave, sounding a dead march with empty pots, trailing our tobacco-pipes instead of pikes, and spew out wine instead of tears.

Enter Peg, Jane, and Anne, as to the tavern.

HARRY. Did not I tell you they would come.

CAPTAIN. What come you for now?

JANE. Not to complain or chide, but to desire your assistance to our designs.

WILL. Let your tongues and tails assist you.

PEG. No, our wits and honesty shall assist us.

CAPTAIN. Pray Jove you have either.

HARRY. Well, let us hear your designs.

ANNE. It is to get us rich husbands.

CAPTAIN. Sister Peg, tell me truly, is the design so honest, and honourable as only to get a rich husband.

PEG. There is no deceit in the end, but only in the way or means.

CAPTAIN. Come, let us go, for perchance our sisters' honest wits may get us honourable means to live with.

Exeunt.

SCENE VI

Enter Lady [Prudence], and her Second Suitor.

SUITOR.   Madam, I was here some little while ago, to tender
my duty to you; but hearing you were not in a pleasing
humour, I durst not venture to present my suit, for there is
a nick of time for lovers to speed.

PRUDENCE.   Sir, I perceive you are well learned in old observations.

SUITOR.   As for learning of all kinds and sorts, I defy it, in so
much that I cannot read the horn-book;[1] neither am I able
to remember the relation of any discourse, if there be
words in it that consist but of two syllables.

PRUDENCE.   How will you make love then?

SUITOR.   Thus madam, I love you with all my heart.

PRUDENCE.   What jointure[2] will you make me?

SUITOR.   Love.

PRUDENCE.   What maintenance will you give me?

SUITOR.   Love.

PRUDENCE.   Can love feed, clothe and maintain me?

SUITOR.   Love is the true elixir, and above all price, being
above gold; it is a creator, madam.

PRUDENCE.   If your love be a creator, then my love shall be
your creature.

Exit Prudence, Suitor solus.

SUITOR.   The Devil himself cannot work upon a woman's
nature.

Enter the Lady [Prudence], and a third Suitor.

SUITOR.   Madam, I hear you are rich.

---

1   horn-book] A sheet of paper with the alphabet written on it (occasionally accompanied by the 10 digits and/or the Lord's Prayer), covered with a protective thin
sheet of translucent horn, used to teach the rudiments of language.
2   Jointure] Marriage portion allotted to the bride on the wedding day.

PRUDENCE.   What then sir?

SUITOR.   And I am poor.

PRUDENCE.   What then?

SUITOR.   Therefore I desire you would be pleased to marry me.

PRUDENCE.   For what?

SUITOR.   To mend my fortune.

PRUDENCE.   I am no cobbler, sir.

Exit Prudence, Suitor solus.

SUITOR.   The Devil take all women's tongues, for they make men fools.

ACT III

SCENE I

Enter Harry, and Doctor Cure-all.

HARRY. Doctor Cure-all, hearing of your fame, hath caused me to send for you, to assist me with your help.

DOCTOR. What is your disease?

HARRY. That you must tell me; but my pain lies in my bones.

DOCTOR. I understand your disease; you must be put to a diet, and you must sweat, and bathe, and something else, if need require it.

HARRY. I hope I have not the pox, Doctor?

DOCTOR. You may say it is a cold, or so; but do you not feel a tenderness in your nose, or a weakness in your legs?

HARRY. My legs are somewhat weak.

DOCTOR. Do you spit much?

HARRY. Sometimes, but not much.

DOCTOR. It were well if you did; for that evacuation is good for young men.

[Harry] gives him a fee.

DOCTOR. By no means sir.

HARRY. Pray Doctor take it.

DOCTOR. Well sir, I shall prescribe some remedies.

HARRY. I shall come to your house, and visit you sometimes, Doctor.

DOCTOR. You shall be welcome sir; if I am not mistaken, your name is Mr. Sensible.

HARRY. It is so sir, your servant Doctor.

Exit Doctor.

Enter Captain and Will to Harry.

CAPTAIN. Harry, it seems you are sick, for we met the Doctor; but what says he to thee.

HARRY. He says, I have the pox.

WILL. A plague of him, but he hath the money.

HARRY. I lent him two pieces upon interest.

CAPTAIN. For the hopes of thy cure: but Will Fullwit, have you got your sister into the Sergeant's service?

WILL. Yes, and he likes her service very well.

CAPTAIN. But Harry, how doth your sister's design go on?

HARRY. Faith slowly; for this is the first time I ever saw the Doctor, but I hope it will come to a good issue in time; but how far is your sister's design gone?

CAPTAIN. So far as I am almost ready to summon him to a Spiritual Court,[1] and yet I have neither spoken to, nor seen the usurer Get-all; but when a business is well laid, it is half done.

HARRY. But if it be to appear before the Spiritual Court, it will be cast forth.

CAPTAIN. I will warrant you I shall get such a judge, as will end the cause on my side; but both of you must be assistants; wherefore let us go to Dick Traveller, where we shall meet my Lieutenant, and Cornet, whom I have well instructed.

Enter Dick, Lieutenant and Cornet.

CAPTAIN. O, have you prevented us; are you ready for the design?

DICK. Yes.

CAPTAIN. But do you understand the cause well?

DICK. So well as I shall not need any further instruction; but where's my fee?

CAPTAIN. But stay, the cause is not ended; for though a bribe go before, a fee comes after.

LIEUTENANT. If judges and lawyers should not be fee'd before causes were decided, they would not be so rich as they are;

---

1 Spiritual Court] The ecclesiastical court designed to prosecute moral and spiritual offenses—it was possible to prosecute the putative father of an illegitimate child for money or other support for the mother and child, though success varied greatly.

but Doctors usually have their fees after their prescriptions and advice; wherefore, Will Fullwit, that must be; Doctor Feel-pulse must not be fee'd beforehand.

CAPTAIN. I only fear Will is not learned enough to play the part of a Doctor of physic.

WILL. Never fear me, for I shall out-argue the college.

DICK. Harry, and you Lieutenant, and Cornet must act as under-officers and clerks.

CORNET. Let Harry act the part of a clerk, and leave us to be under-officers.

CAPTAIN. No, no, Harry must be a pleader; but I never thought soldiers should turn judges, and lawyers before now.

DICK. Why not as well as priests turn soldiers.

CAPTAIN. Come, let us go about this great affair.

Enter Peg.

CAPTAIN. Peg, have you got your child ready?

PEG. Yes.

WILL. Have you confidence to outface the court?

PEG. I can face the court; but I fear I cannot outface or out-case usurer Get-all.

CAPTAIN. Never fear it, Peg.

PEG. Pray Jove we speed, for the good of the commonwealth of Cavaliers.

CAPTAIN. Well Peg, be ready against I send for you.

Exeunt Men.

Enter Anne, and Informer, to Peg.

ANNE. How is your design like to prove?

PEG. Well I hope; but Mrs. Informer, have you seen Jane Full-wit since she went to be a lawyer's clerk?

INFORMER. I have, and she told me, that her master is much pleased with her service; but I going often to visit his clerk, the Sergeant having notice of it watched when I was with him, and was very angry, and said I was such a bawd as corrupted all the apprentices, and lawyer's clerks in the city. But I fear for all your industry, your designs will not come to that effect you desire.

PEG.   Why, what hinders them?

INFORMER.   Why, those three rich men, that I informed you of, do eagerly woo the old Lady Riches.

JANE.   Are the men young, or old?

INFORMER.   Neither; they are of a middle age.

ANNE.   Then she will never marry any of them; for old women love young men; besides, she can marry but one.

PEG.   Come, come, it is impossible, but we shall be preferred before the old lady.

INFORMER.   I wish you may.

PEG.   I will warrant you, we shall have good success if you act your part well.

INFORMER.   Never fear me, for I shall out-act you all.

PEG.   Come, let us go to the child, to put dry cloth to it, and to wrap it warm with a mantle, for fear it catch cold; for if it get cold, my brother will be angry.

Exit Women.

Get-all the Usurer sitting casting up accounts.

Enter his man Roger.

ROGER.   Will your worship give me leave to speak freely to you?

GET-ALL.   Yes, Roger, freely.

ROGER.   I wonder your worship will starve your life to fill your purse.

GET-ALL.   O Roger, when the purse is full, the life cannot starve for want.

ROGER.   'Tis true, he that is rich may eat if he have a stomach; but you will neither eat nor sleep, but wear out your life in casting up the accounts of your riches, and yet have not an heir to leave it to.

GET-ALL. Wealth never wants heirs.

ROGER. Indeed such heirs, that will give no thanks for what they do receive?

GET-ALL. But I can make the meritorious my heirs.

ROGER. You may make heirs, but not merit, sir.

GET-ALL. Do you think there are not men of merit?

ROGER. Faith sir, merit died many years since, and left no posterity.

Enter Tom his other man.

TOM. Sir, there is one Captain Valour desires to speak with your worship.

GET-ALL. These poor Cavaliers haunt me like spirits, they will not let me rest in peace.

ROGER. Faith sir, they are like hounds, that hunt an aftergame.

GET-ALL. But they shall not catch my wealth; for they have no lands to mortgage, nor goods to pawn.

ROGER. I believe they have not anything to pawn or mortgage, unless it be their honesties.

GET-ALL. But poor honesty will pay no debts; wherefore tell the Captain, I am not to be spoken with.

Exit Servant [Tom].

ROGER. But your worship said, you would leave your wealth to men of merit.

GET-ALL. Yes, Roger, I may leave them my wealth when I die; but not give it them whilst I live.

ROGER. But if the Cavaliers be men of merit, they may be starved before you are like to die; for you are not fifty years of age, and healthful and temperate, whereas they are weak with want and disorders.

GET-ALL. Want and disorders seldom go together; wherefore we'll endeavour to get the old Lady Riches.

ROGER. What, to be disorderly?

GET-ALL. No, to be rich.

ROGER. But would you marry this old Lady Riches in earnest?

GET-ALL. Yes; but I would not see her before I am married, for fear I should dislike her; and that would disquiet my mind between two passions, dislike and covetousness.

ROGER. But you have a mass of wealth already, so in my judgment you should desire no more.

GET-ALL. You are a fool; for I would be as rich as the Indies, and then I should be more than half as rich as the King of Spain.

ROGER. But what would you do with it, if you had it?

GET-ALL. I would fight with the Great Turk.[1]

ROGER. But you said, that you would give your wealth to men of merit.

GET-ALL. Why so I shall, if I give it to valiant soldiers, to fight against the Turk.

ROGER. But would your worship head your own army?

GET-ALL. Yes.

ROGER. Truly that would be a kind of a miracle; for I never heard of an usurer that was valiant.

Enter the Servant [Tom] again.

TOM. Sir, Captain Valour is without still, he will not go away.

GET-ALL. I cannot speak with him.

TOM. He bids me tell you, that he doth not come to borrow money, for he knows you will lend him none; but he says, he came to inform you of a business that highly concerns you.

GET-ALL. Well, bring him in; but be sure Roger and Tom, that both of you be in the next room, for I do not love to be with a soldier alone.

---

1 King of Spain ... Great Turk] Both Spain and the Turks were traditional and long-time enemies of England (on both religious and political grounds). Both rulers were masters of enormous wealth and substantial empires during the seventeenth century. Get-all is fantasizing about a ridiculously huge sum of money to spend on a near-impossible exercise.

ROGER. But you dare trust yourself at the head of an army.

GET-ALL. Yes, yes, but that is against the Turk; but hold your prating and send in the Captain.

Exit Roger [and Tom].

Enter Captain.

CAPTAIN. Mr. Get-all, I am come to inform you, that there is a young gentlewoman brought to bed.

GET-ALL. What is that to me.

CAPTAIN. It is to you, if it be true what they say, which is, that you got it.

GET-ALL. If she can prove I got it, I will not only keep the child, but marry the woman; but I did believe I was always insufficient.

CAPTAIN. You speak as an honest gentleman, and I shall tell her what you say.

Exit Captain.

Enter Roger.

GET-ALL. Roger, I am provided of an heir, for I have a child laid to my charge.

ROGER. Of the Captain's begetting.

GET-ALL. I believe so; but the wench lays it to my charge.

ROGER. Faith sir, I never saw anything like a woman, near your worship, since I came to be your servant, which is above twenty years; as for your old cook-maid, she is nothing like a woman.

GET-ALL. Why, what is she like then?

ROGER. Like a spirit, whose substance is wasted in hell-fire.

GET-ALL. Well Roger, but I must be careful to avoid this wench's plot against me, and there is no way, that I can perceive, to avoid it, but to marry as speedily as I can; wherefore carry the old Lady Riches that present, and let her into my chamber, and if it be possible speak to herself and woo her for me.

ROGER. Faith sir, I am as bad a wooer as yourself; for I never wooed any woman but your cook-maid for a breakfast, or to make me a bag-pudding; and how such kind of wooing will fit a lady, I cannot tell.

GET-ALL. But you can tell her, how rich I am.

ROGER. That I can, and in my conscience that is as good a wooing-plea as any is.

GET-ALL. And you may tell her that one of my age is fitter to match with one of her age, than a younger man.

ROGER. Those two arguments will spoil all, especially that of mentioning her age, for women cannot endure to hear of their age, were they as old as Methuselah.

GET-ALL. Well, use what arguments you shall think fit.

ROGER. Shall I woo as the young gallants, in court language?

GET-ALL. What language is that?

ROGER. Fine phrases, and mode-expressions, which is a mixture with French words, and high compliments.

GET-ALL. How high?

ROGER. As high as nonsense, which is beyond understanding.

GET-ALL. Prithee use what language or expressions you will.

ROGER. But put the case I should woo so courtly, as to get her for myself?

GET-ALL. If you do Roger, I shall wish you joy.

ROGER. I thank you sir.

Exit Roger

Enter Tom his other Man.

TOM. Sir, there is a young gentlewoman come in a coach, who desires to speak with your worship.

GET-ALL. I'll pawn my life it is she, that desires to lay her bastard to my charge.

TOM. Certainly, she is none of that trade, for she is come in a coach.

GET-ALL. Why a hackney woman may ride in a hackney-coach; there is no law against it, Tom.

TOM. But in my conscience this gentlewoman looks as modestly, as if she were honest.

GET-ALL. But a modest countenance is oftentimes made use of only to cover the face of adultery.

TOM. Then you will not speak with her?

GET-ALL. No, for there is antipathy between me and womankind, since this accusation.

Tom was going out, and returns back.

TOM. Sir, here is the Captain.

Enter Captain.

GET-ALL. What would you have now?

CAPTAIN. I am come to summon you to the Spiritual Court.

GET-ALL. I shall obey; but how shall I find the Court, for I was never there?

CAPTAIN. I will go but to the next house to speak with a friend, and I will come and direct you to the place.

GET-ALL. I pray do.

Exit Captain.

Enter Roger.

GET-ALL. I am glad you are not gone to the lady, for I am summoned to the Spiritual Court.

ROGER. The Captain's coming made me stay, but what are you summoned for, a bag of money?

GET-ALL. Indeed that is the design, but the pretence is, for getting the child, I told you was laid to my charge.

ROGER. Why, this is the misery of wealth, a man can never be quiet; and you being very rich, it will be the policy of the Spiritual Court, to make you maintain all the whores, and their bastards, in the city.

GET-ALL. Like enough.

ROGER.   And if there be an overplus, you may leave that to the meritorious; so then you will maintain vice in your life, and virtue when you are dead.

GET-ALL.   But surely my innocence[1] will defend me from the injury of injustice.

ROGER.   Faith, injustice is too prevalent for innocence, in these days.

GET-ALL.   Well, let us go, for I must obey the laws.

ROGER.   But sir, you are not provided of lawyers to plead on your side.

GET-ALL.   I shall not need them, for I can declare my own innocence.

Exeunt Get-all and Servant.

Enter as in a court of justice, Dick, as prime judge of the Spiritual Court, the Lieutenant and Cornet as two clerks, Harry Sensible as a lawyer, or pleader, for the plaintiff; Will Fullwit as a physician; Mrs. Peg Valorosa the plaintiff; Informer, as a midwife and witness; and Captain Valorous as their friend; when all sit in order.

Enter Get-all and Roger.

HARRY.   Most reverend judge, here is a gentlewoman come, who desires justice.

DICK.   What is her cause?

HARRY.   Her cause is, that she being a virtuous young woman, hath behaved herself modestly, and hath kept a good reputation in the world (which all her neighbours know) until such time as this Mr. Get-all got her with child, which child he will neither own nor keep, nor marry the woman.

DICK.   Have you any witnesses?

HARRY.   We have such a witness as the law allows of, which is a midwife.

GET-ALL.   I require the witness to be heard.

---

1   innocence] innocency F1

DICK. Will you witness that the child is Mr. Get-all's.

INFORMER. I will witness the words of the labouring woman.

DICK. Declare them.

INFORMER. About twelve a clock at night I being in bed, and fast asleep, there comes a man, and raps, and raps, and — raps at the door, as if it had been for life, which in truth proved so; for it was to fetch me to bring a sweet babe into the world; but I hearing one rap so hard, I was afraid, my door, being but a rotten door, should be broke to pieces; I ran to the window to ask, who knocked so hard; but the man knocked on, and I called out; which knocking and calling took up half an hour's time; but at last, my tongue being louder than the clapper, he heard me then; I asked him what was his business? he said, I must go presently to a young gentlewoman that was in labour; upon which summons I did rise and put on my bodice, but did not half lace them; also my petticoats, but did not tie them fast enough; for when I came into the middle of the broad street, my coats fell quite down from my hips, but as good luck would have it, it was dark night, but the ill fortune was, that my coats fell down, when I was striding over the broad kennel, in which posture I stood a great time, until the man helped me over; but my coats were all wet.

GET-ALL. But what is all this to the confession of the labouring woman?

She answers angrily.[1]

INFORMER. It is of concern; for circumstance is partly a declaring of truth.

DICK. You say true Mistress, wherefore go on.

INFORMER. But as I said —— stay, I have forgot; where did I leave?

CAPTAIN. You left at the wet coats, Mistress.

INFORMER. 'Tis very true, I humbly thank you sir; the coats, as I said, being wet, I was loath to put them on, not only

---

1 angrily] angerly F1

for fear of catching cold, but for fear I should endanger the woman's miscarriage by my retardments;[1] so I went with never a coat on me, the man carried them for me; but the night was pretty warm, so that I got no cold, I thank Jupiter; but being more nimble, as being more light, I was soon at the house of the labouring woman, whom I found in painful throes, and she groaned most pitifully; and I comforted her, and prayed her to have patience, and at last she was brought to bed of a very lusty boy.

GET-ALL. But what did the gentlewoman confess?

INFORMER. What gentlewoman?

GET-ALL. This gentlewoman.

INFORMER. This gentlewoman hath confessed that she was never got with child, nor never had a child, but what Mr. Get-all begot; and this I will take my oath of.

DICK. How can you clear yourself Mr. Get-all?

GET-ALL. I will take my oath that I never did see this gentlewoman, about whom I am accused, in my life; and I have a servant here that can witness for me.

Roger comes forward.

DICK. What can you witness?

ROGER. I can witness that I have lived with my master these twenty years, in all which time I did never see my master converse with anything like a woman.

DICK. Doth your master keep no servant-maid?

ROGER. There is one we call the cook-maid, but whether she be maid or woman, I'll take my oath I know not.

DICK. Then your master may converse with women you know not of.

ROGER. But I will swear my master did never converse with this gentlewoman that hath the child.

GET-ALL. And I will take my oath, as I said, that I never did so much as see her before now.

---

1 retardments] lateness

CAPTAIN. But may it please you, most reverend judge, this gentlewoman hath seen him.

GET-ALL. But the bare sight of me could not get her with child.

CAPTAIN. That is to be proved; wherefore we require so much justice of this reverend judge, that Mr. Feel-pulse, a most learned and expert doctor of physic, may prove it by argumentation.

DICK. Let Mr. Doctor prove it.

Will steps forward.

WILL. Then be it known to this most reverend judge, and to Mr. Get-all, and the rest of this assembly, that our famous doctor is of opinion, (as also the heads of our schools and colleges) that the production of animal kind, is by an incorporeal motion; and the famous doctor is also of opinion, that the soul of Man slides from the stomach to the heel, and in that journey makes a production: and all the Platonics[1] do affirm, that there may be a conjunction of souls, although the bodies be at a far distance; and I am absolutely of that opinion; and that the idea of a man, by the help of a strong imagination, may beget a child; which is sufficiently proved; for she seeing Mr. Get-all enter into the house of Mr. Inkhorn the scrivener, viewed his person so exactly, that when she was in bed, a strong imagination seized on her, by which she conceived a child.

GET-ALL. It seems the child was begot like the plague, by conceit.

DICK. You say true, Mr. Get-all; wherefore you must marry the woman, own the child, and keep them both.

GET-ALL. Is there no avoiding your sentence, Mr. Judge?

JUDGE. No, the decree is passed.

---

1 Platonics] Philosophers adhering to the doctrines of Plato, in which the soul and the body are separate entities and subject to different forms of love. The concept of Platonic love was very much in vogue at the court of Queen Henrietta Maria before the war; Cavendish here is taking the idea of souls loving one another on a spiritual (rather than a physical) plane to its logical (and ridiculous) extreme here.

GET-ALL. Why then as she was got with child by conceit, so I will marry her by conceit.

JUDGE. But you must take her, and her child home, and maintain them.

GET-ALL. Cannot I maintain them by conceit?

JUDGE. No, that must be done corporeally.[1]

GET-ALL. If there be no remedy, I must be content; come my conceited or Platonic wife and child, let us go home.

ALL. We wish you all happiness.

Exeunt.

SCENE II

Enter the Lady [Prudence] and a fourth Suitor.

SUITOR. Madam, I suppose my name is unknown to you?

PRUDENCE. 'Tis probable sir; for I never saw you before.

SUITOR. Then I'll tell you, madam, my name is, Monsieur Vanity.

PRUDENCE. Your name shows that your humour is foolish, and your actions prodigal.

SUITOR. My humour is noble, madam, and my actions generous; for I usually cast away a hundred pounds at dice, and run away a hundred pounds at a race, and give away a hundred pounds at a visit to a mistress.

PRUDENCE. This last kind of prodigality has some resemblance to generosity; but yet it is as different from generosity, as a bribe is from an uninterested gift. But pray sir, give me leave to ask you, what design brought you hither to me?

SUITOR. A very good design, madam; for I being vain, and you rich, t'would be very convenient we two should join as man and wife, that one might maintain the other.

PRUDENCE. Alas sir, the wife would soon die in her husband's

---

1 corporeally] corporally F1

arms; for riches consume in vanity; therefore, I will as soon marry death, as you.[1]

Exit Prudence.

SUITOR.[2] Death take her, if I cannot get her.

Enter three Gentlewomen to the Lady [Prudence].

PRUDENCE. I am glad you are come to release me from the importunity of my suitors.

1 GENTLEWOMAN. You are in a good condition, madam, that you can have lovers that seek you, when as we for want of wealth, are forced to seek them.

2 GENTLEWOMAN. You mean husbands, madam, for lovers are never sought, because they are never lost; for a lover will always be at the tail of his mistress.

3 GENTLEWOMAN. I wish I had as many as would make up a train.

Exit Suitor.

Enter her Father Save-all.

SAVE-ALL. Daughter, have you made your choice of a husband, since you have so many suitors?

PRUDENCE. No truly sir, for the number confounds my choice, or rather there is no choice in all the number, by reason none exceeds the other, but they are all fools alike.

SAVE-ALL. Indeed daughter, if you be so long a-choosing, you will be past choice yourself.

PRUDENCE. I had rather be old with judgment, than young with folly; and since you have been pleased to trust to my discretion, I would not willingly betray that trust, by the haste of my choice.

---

1   The SD "Exit Lady" appears here, but I have removed it for consistency's sake.
2   Suitor] Suitor Solus F1

SAVE-ALL.   You speak well, daughter; Heaven grant you do well.

PRUDENCE.   But pray sir give me leave to ask you one question.

SAVE-ALL.   What's that?

PRUDENCE.   I would fain know, whether my lovers do first address their suits to you, or to me?

SAVE-ALL.   Their suits they address first to you; but their inquiries are made first to me; to wit, what portion I would give you, and whether I intend to settle all my estate upon you.

PRUDENCE.   It seems they consider my wealth before my person.

SAVE-ALL.   Yes, and all wooers do the like.

PRUDENCE.   But not lovers sir.

SAVE-ALL.   Yes, yes, for they woo first, marry next, and love last.

Exit Father [Save-all].

SCENE III

*Enter the fifth Suitor to the Lady [Prudence],
being an ancient man.*

SUITOR.   Madam, I see you are a beauty, and report speaks you virtuous and wise; which if so, I hope you'll choose an ancient lover before a young one.

PRUDENCE.   No question sir, but an ancient lover expresses more constancy in his love, than a young one doth; but ancient love requires a great deal of time. And my father may die before I make my choice.

SUITOR.   You mistake me, madam, I mean an ancient man that loves you.

PRUDENCE.   There is great difference between an ancient man, and an ancient lover: but sir, by your discourse I perceive you pretend to be a lover.

SUITOR. My love is not pretended; for I do really love you.

PRUDENCE. How can I know that?

SUITOR. By proof; for I'll not require any portion with you, since I am rich enough without; nay, I will not only take you without a portion, but make you mistress of all my wealth, in so much that I will freely give you all I am worth; and I wish I were worth millions for your sake.

PRUDENCE. Sir, you express more love in your gifts, than all my young suitors in their words; and if you will confirm your promise to my father, which you have now made to me, I shall accept of you for a husband, and promise you, to be an honest and loving wife.

He kisses her hand.

SUITOR. Let us both go to your father, and conclude the bargain.

ACT IV

SCENE I

Enter Lawyer [Sergeant Plead-all] and his She-Clerk [Jane].

SERGEANT.   Is Doctor Cure-all so industrious about the old Lady Riches?

JANE.[1] Yes sir, he was very busy in preparing of cordials, ointments, and such things; and was angry that I came with a message from you; for he bid me be gone; for the lady, he said, could not hear love-messages, she was so full of sciatic pain and gout; but the old lady did favour me, and chided the doctor for bidding me to be gone; for she would have heard my message, when her sides were anointed, and her gouty toe plastered.

SERGEANT.   And did you stand by, till she was anointed?

JANE.   Yes sir, for she did desire me to help to anoint her sides, whilst the doctor laid a plaster to her toe.

SERGEANT.   And now did she like your service?

JANE.   So well, sir, as she said, she was never better chafed and rubbed in her life; I suppose it was for your sake.

SERGEANT.   But when I am married, I shall not allow her my clerk to anoint her sides, although she be so old to go upon crutches.

Exit Jack [Jane] Clerk.

Enter another Clerk.

CLERK.   Sir, there is a client without, desires to speak with you; and there is a gentleman without, that doth rail bitterly.

SERGEANT.   For what?

CLERK.   Because his lawsuit went against him; he says, that all the poor Cavaliers are not only undone by the wars, but also by the lawyers.

---

1   Jane] The speech prefix 'Jack' is used in F1; I have altered it for clarity.

SERGEANT.   These poor Cavaliers are very troublesome.

CLERK.   Alas, their losses make them impatient.

SERGEANT.   They are so poor, that lawyers cannot gain by them; wherefore, we are for the other party; who are so rich, that 'tis fit their purses should be emptied.

CLERK.   But if they get their suits, sir, the poor Cavaliers pay the charges.

SERGEANT.   Hold your prating, and bid Jack Clerk come to me.

Enter Jack [Jane] Clerk.

SERGEANT.   Have you writ those deeds out?

JANE.   Yes sir.

SERGEANT.   And have you copied out those cases that I am to plead for, and against?

JANE.   Yes sir.

SERGEANT.   'Tis well done.

JANE.   Sir you are pleased to seem to favour me.

SERGEANT.   I do really love thee, and will do thee any favour I can.

JANE.   Then I desire you would be pleased to plead a cause that concerns a kinswoman of mine.

SERGEANT.   That I will to the best of my power; but what is the case?

JANE.   Why sir, I have a kinswoman who is well born, but poor, and gentlewoman; but a gentleman being in love with her, and she not condescending to his unlawful desire, hath taken her away by force, and keeps her by force.

SERGEANT.   Have you witness?

JANE.   Yes sir, I have two witnesses.

SERGEANT.   That is sufficient; let them be ready at the next sessions.

JANE.   But sir, I desire not to appear as plaintiff, for I have got another gentleman to be plaintiff; and my friends are without, sir, if you please to see them.

SERGEANT.   Well, call them.

Enter the Lieutenant and Cornet.

SERGEANT.   Gentlemen, I shall serve you as well as I can.

LIEUTENANT. & CORNET.   We thank you sir.

Exit Sergeant.

Enter Dick, Will, Harry and Captain.

JANE.   Gentlemen, you are welcome.

WILL.   We are come to know if we shall have a hearing?

JANE.   My master hath promised to plead on our behalf.

HARRY.   We desire no more.

JANE.   But I am to inform this society, that there is a very rich old lady, (a widow) who these three rich men court; the usurer did woo her, and the lawyer and physician do woo her; and if any one of you could cozen these three of the lady, it would be a masterpiece.

HARRY.   But should not any one of us cozen ourselves or she cozen us to marry her? for she is so old, that there is no hope of posterity.

DICK.   Why shall we desire posterity, so long as we are poor? and if any one of us should ever come to be so happy as to be rich, if he hath no children, and chance to die, let him leave his wealth amongst the society of poor Cavaliers.

ALL SPEAK.   Content. Content.

LIEUTENANT.   But which of us shall address himself to this old lady?

HARRY.   Dick Traveller is most likely to speed.

DICK.   I have white hairs; wherefore I am confident I shall be refused.

CAPTAIN.   The truth is, the only man that is probable to speed, is Harry Sensible; for he hath a young smooth face, and old women love young smooth faced men a'life.

HARRY.   Yes, but a young man doth not love an old woman; wherefore she is a fitter match for Dick than for me.

WILL.   Harry is in the right, Dick is the fittest match for her; but the difficulty will be, how to make the match, for we shall find it more difficult for all us men to cozen one woman, than for one woman to cozen all us men.

LIEUTENANT.   It is impossible; wherefore let us never endeavour it.

CORNET.   But we will never lose any design for want of endeavour.

JANE.   I will tell you my masters, how to compass this design.

DICK.   How?

JANE.   Harry shall put himself into a woman's habit, and Madam Informer who is acquainted with the lady, shall prefer Harry to be her chambermaid, where he may have time and opportunity to commend Dick, and to bring him acquainted with her.

WILL.   He may do some good in that, and perchance not.

JANE.   It is but trying.

HARRY.   I like the design so well, as I am resolved to become a chambermaid.

WILL.   But we shall want thy company in the meantime.

HARRY.   No, no, I am confident I shall get leave sometimes to go abroad, or find some ways or other to slip out.

LIEUTENANT.   But you cannot change your habit suddenly.

HARRY.   I shall not have occasion, for you all know me.

DICK.   Come, come, let us about this business.

JACK.   But first you must go with me to hear the cause tried.

ALL SPEAK.   Content, content.

Exeunt.

Enter Roger, solus.

ROGER.   If my young mistress should have a perfect idea of me, and then a strong imagination, she might prove with child again, and so my master would be a platonic cuckold.

Enter Get-all.

GET-ALL.   Roger, where is my platonic wife and child?

ROGER.   In the chamber with the milk-nurse.

GET-ALL. My family is well increased since I have been a platonic husband and father.

ROGER. I hope your Worship will not want heirs to inherit your wealth?

GET-ALL. No, no, I cannot want heirs, the way being so easy to get them.

ROGER. But hath not your Worship a mind to get her with child, after a corporeal manner?

GET-ALL. Faith Roger, she is tempting, being young and handsome; but if I should get her with child as our forefathers got us, I fear this learned age will punish me, either with death or intolerable fines.

ROGER. But if there be no witness, they cannot prove it; for this platonic son and heir of your Worship's, appears as if it had been got by a corporeal action.

GET-ALL. You say true; wherefore call your mistress.

The while he walks, enter Mistress Peg.

GET-ALL. My imaginary wife, how doth our imaginary son?

PEG. Very well, sir.

GET-ALL. But doth he corporeally suck?

PEG. Yes sir.

GET-ALL. I wonder at that; but my greatest wonder is, how that an incorporeal conception, should come to be a corporeal child!

PEG. 'Tis like spirits that take bodies, sir.

GET-ALL. But may I not lawfully get you with child after a corporeal manner?

PEG. Yes surely, sir.

GET-ALL. Then let us go to bed, and try if I can get a child after the old corporeal way, for I never know when this child was gotten.

PEG. But I must be ceremoniously married first.

GET-ALL. Hang ceremony, those children never come to good that are got with ceremony.

PEG. But I cannot lie with you corporeally, unless you honestly marry me.

GET-ALL. But I tell you, I did not know when I got this child which I am forced to own.

PEG. 'Tis true, sir; but that was begot by your idea, and my imagination, and not personally; wherefore, if you desire to lie with me, you must first marry me, otherwise the law will severely punish us, and they would be glad we should give them that occasion, that they might take away your wealth.

GET-ALL. Faith, thou shall rather breed by conceit, than I marry really; but if we must not lie together corporeally, may not we kiss corporeally?

PEG. Truly sir, I did never kiss any man but in the way of a civil salute.

GET-ALL. But did not my idea and your imagination kiss?

PEG. Yes sir, but not corporeally.

GET-ALL. Faith, I have a natural desire to thee; but I dare not marry thee, for fear I should be made a cuckold, as I have been made a father.

PEG. Truly I am very chaste, and shall make a very honest wife; and if you will promise to marry me, I will discover by whom you have been deceived.

GET-ALL. If you can prove yourself honest, I will.

PEG. Then know sir, this child which is laid to your charge, is none of mine, but a bastard of my brother's, Captain Valour; but by reason my brother was ruined in the Civil Wars, and I having lost my portion in his ruin, I had not means to maintain me honestly, according to my quality; wherefore, hearing you were a very worthy person, and rich, and an unmarried man, I desired my brother's assistance in the design of getting you to be my husband; but the design could not take effect if we had not counterfeited a Spiritual Court and judge, which judge was Mr. Traveller; and the doctor Mr. Will Fullwit; and the lawyer was Mr. Sensible; and my brothers, Lieutenant and Major, witnesses; all gallant valiant men, but poor Cavaliers; so that the design was honest, but the management was full of deceit.

GET-ALL. But what was she that was the midwife.

PEG. An honest ancient gentlewoman, whose husband was killed in the wars.

GET-ALL. Well, since you have so ingenuously told me the truth, I will marry thee for thy honest wit; for he's a fool that will marry a fool.

Enter judges as in a Court of Judicature, and Sergeant Plead-all[1] as a pleader at the bar, and his clerk with a bag of papers; also Harry Sensible as the defendant, and Will Fullwit and Dick Traveller as Witnesses, the Captain as a Plaintiff, and the Lieutenant and Ancient as Witnesses.

SERGEANT. May it please your lordships, I am here to plead in my client's behalf against Mr. Sensible, who against the laws of honour, honesty, and civil government, hath a young gentlewoman of good birth and education (but poor) in his keeping, not by the gentlewoman's (or friends) consent, but by constraint and force, enclosing her in a chamber, under locks and bolts, lest she should escape from him.

JUDGE. Where are your witnesses?

LIEUTENANT. Here my lords.

JUDGE. Will you both swear these accusations for a truth?

LIEUTENANT. We are ready to swear whensoever the book is offered.

JUDGE. What says the defendant?

HARRY. My lords, I will confess the truth, but I desire justice, and that my accusation against Sergeant Plead-all, may be heard.

SERGEANT. Good my lords, grant his request; for as I fear not what can be said against me.

JUDGE. We grant his request.

HARRY. Then my lords, I freely confess that I have such a gentlewoman in my keeping, as I am accused, and do keep her under lock and key; not for fear she should leave me, but for fear some man should steal her away from me; for in this age men are like hungry wolves, seeking to devour

---

1   Plead-all] Barrister F1

the virginity and reputation of young women: but this young gentlewoman who I do so carefully keep, is my own natural sister, which these two worthy gentlemen, Mr. Fullwit and Mr. Traveller, will witness; besides, I can bring all my neighbours that will witness the same; and since Sergeant Plead-all hath endeavoured to disgrace me, not only before your lordships, but before a court full of people; I think it not unmeet, for me to declare to your lordships, that Sergeant Plead-all hath at this present kept in his house a gentlewoman, as a servant, in man's clothes, whose birth and breeding is better than his own.

SERGEANT. My lords, I deny his impeachment; and if he can prove that I have a woman in man's clothes, that is a household servant of mine, I will marry her, were she an old witch.

HARRY. My lords, this assembly is sufficient witness of what he hath said, as also what I have said; and to prove what I say is true, here is the gentlewoman who serves him as his clerk, in man's clothes, she is sister to Mr. Fullwit, which he and others will witness, and she herself confesses.

JANE. My lords, I do confess I am a woman, and out of love to Sergeant Plead-all did take this disguise, which I hope is pardonable, since it is not a breach of the laws of the kingdom, whatsoever it may be in modesty.

SERGEANT. How is this! My clerk a woman! and must be my wife! I am finely cozened i'faith!

HARRY. We beseech your lordships to give your judgment.

JUDGES. Our judgment is, that you are free, and the Sergeant must marry his she-clerk.

Exeunt.

SCENE II

Enter Father [Save-all], with his daughter [Prudence].

PRUDENCE.   Pray sir, tell me whether you approve of my choice?

SAVE-ALL.   To speak truly, daughter, you have chosen very wisely; but how your youth will agree with age, I cannot tell.

PRUDENCE.   Never fear it sir, for I shall love age in a husband, better than youth in myself.

SAVE-ALL.   Well, Heaven bless you.

Enter a messenger from the young suitors.

MESSENGER.   Sir, report says, that the lady your daughter, is to be married to an ancient man, to the great disgrace of her other suitors' youth, beauty, and bravery; and therefore they desire, that before she marries, she would be pleased to give them all a public audience.

SAVE-ALL.   Daughter, answer this gentleman.

PRUDENCE.   Sir, pray tell them, that I cannot civilly deny their request, in case they'd be pleased to give me leave to make a public answer.

MESS.   No question, madam, but they will, and I shall inform them of what you say.

Exeunt.

ACT V

SCENE I

Enter Mrs. Jane Fullwit in her woman's habit,
and Sergeant Plead-all.

SERGEANT. Well Mistress, your wit and your person hath not
only excused your deceit, but I am so in love with you, that
I would not but have been deceived for all the world.

JANE. Sir, with your pardon, there is one more deceived
besides yourself, and another like to be.

SERGEANT. Who be those?

JANE. He that is deceived, is Get-all the usurer, and he that
shall be deceived is Doctor Cure-all.

SERGEANT. What, my two rivals?

JANE. Yes sir.

SERGEANT. Then they cannot laugh at me.

JANE. If they do, you may laugh at them again.

SERGEANT. I would the old lady was deceived.

JANE. She will in a short time.

SERGEANT. Faith, I find that the Cavaliers are the best
deceivers.

JANE. They have been so oft deceived themselves, that they
have learned by their misfortunes.

SERGEANT. But we will not deceive each other, but go to
your brother to dispatch our marriage.

Exeunt.

Enter Captain, Lieutenant, Cornet, and Will Fullwit, then enter
Harry in a chambermaid's habit.

WILL. Mrs. Harry you are welcome, how doth your good
lady?

She [Harry] makes a curtsy ill-favouredly.

HARRY. My lady at this time is troubled with love in the heart, and gout in the toe.

CAPTAIN. Is Dick Traveller the cause of the love-sick heart?

HARRY. No, it is the lawyer's young clerk.

WILL. He is discovered.

HARRY. Yes, but I will not suffer any to inform her of it.

CORNET. But if her mind be so young, I doubt we may despair of our design.

Enter Dick Traveller.

DICK. Mrs. Harry, give me leave to salute you.

He makes a curtsy, and he salutes him.

DICK. Faith Harry, you kiss like a woman; I pray Jove you be not turned female with wearing a petticoat.

HARRY. If I be, I pray Jove I may not be such a female as my old lady is.

DICK. But how goeth on our design?

HARRY. Fast towards a young man, but slowly towards a gray head.

DICK. What young man?

HARRY. The lawyer's clerk.

DICK. What is she in love with honest Jack? But she is discovered.

HARRY. But she knows not of it, for she is almost desperate; and between every groan of pain, she sighs for love.

DICK. Why, then there is no hope for me.

HARRY. Not unless you are presented in the name of the clerk, and married by candle-light; for she being half blind, will never distinguish which is which.

CAPTAIN. Faith, Harry's counsel is good.

WILL. But if she be as deaf as she is blind, we shall not need to dissemble his name.

DICK. But Harry, do you think she will live long?

HARRY. My only fear is, she will hardly live so long that he may be married to her.

DICK. I hope she is not so desperately sick.

LIEUTENANT. If she should die before Dick is married, we are all undone.

CORNET. If she should, it would be worse than our cashiering.

WILL. Take comfort gentlemen, for old women are such dry and tough meat, that Death cannot set his teeth into them, nor his dart enter them.

CAPTAIN. Will says true; for perchance she may last longer than Dick would have her.

DICK. I would have her live till I am married to her, and then let her die as soon as she will.

HARRY. Well, gentlemen, I dare stay no longer for fear my lady should chide me most grievously.

WILL. Thou art a most grievous rogue.

Exit Harry.

Enter Sergeant and Jane.

WILL. Hey-day, who comes here!

SERGEANT. We are come to have you for a witness to our marriage, since you proved so good a one at the bar.

WILL. Stay so long, till we see an end of our comedy.

SERGEANT. If your comedy be long, I shall not have patience.

CAPTAIN. It shall be short, and you shall have more bridals to accompany you.

Enter Harry.

HARRY. I have been at home with my mistress; but all the plot of Jack Clerk was revealed to her, whilst I was here; O Mr. Plead-all, I cry you mercy, I saw you not.

SERGEANT. Nay, Mrs. Harry pray conceal not anything for my being here; for I thank you, I am now become one of the society.

HARRY. And how do you like of the acquaintance.

SERGEANT. So well, as I would not be a stranger for any other good.

HARRY. I presume Mrs. Jane hath pleased you well.

SERGEANT. So well, as I am confident I shall be happy in my marriage: But how doth the old lady take the discovery of my she-clerk?

HARRY. Faith, as ill as she would take the discovery of her he-chambermaid; the truth is, she hath been in such passions, as she is almost transformed to mummy.

SERGEANT. That she was before the discovery.

HARRY. But now she is more perfect mummy than she was; but I, to comfort her, have promised to bring her a handsome young man, only he is taller and bigger, as being a man; and I did reason with her so long, that I have persuaded her to love a man, rather than a boy.

CAPTAIN. And will she come to reason?

HARRY. She will, upon condition he be a young man.

DICK. But how shall I make myself appear to be a young man?

CORNET. You are not so old, but you may appear in the dark to be a young man.

CAPTAIN. Appear, say you! how the devil can he appear in the dark?

HARRY. Well, for the good of the Commonwealth,[1] I have devised a way how Dick shall appear like a young man to a blind eye.

WILL. Faith, I know no difference between the dark and a blind eye.

HARRY. Hang you, a pox of you all, I meant a dim eye.

DICK. Come, dim or blind, let's hear your design.

HARRY. This is the design, Dick shall first shave as close as may be, and then paint his face, and with a handsome perriwig,[2] and fine clothes, he will appear a young man to an old woman.

WILL. Faith, the paint must be laid on his face as thick as mortar on a wall, otherwise his age will be seen.

CAPTAIN. Not to a dim eye.

---

1 commonwealth] common-weale F1
2 perriwig] A wig, often of long hair, worn by highly fashionable men during the Restoration years.

DICK. Why, I have not such wrinkles in my face as requires much filling up.

HARRY. I will warrant you, that I will get such an artist; that if Dick's wrinkles were as deep as a sawpit, they should be closed up, and his face appear fair and even, if not smooth; wherefore Dick, get a handsome perriwig, and put on your best suit of clothes, and I will send a painter to your chamber; then go to her, for she expects thee, and carry a priest, and some witnesses, and marry her.

WILL. Will not you be there?

HARRY. I cannot, but I have left those in her house that shall conduct you to her; but I must go about my sister's affairs, where I must desire all the company to meet me at Doctor Cure-all's house.

ALL SPEAK. We will not fail you.

DICK. But the Cornet and Lieutenant must go with me to be my witnesses.

HARRY. Take them.

Exeunt.

SCENE II

Enter Doctor and his Man.

DOCTOR. Give me my cloak, for now the clerk being proved a woman, I hope the old lady will accept of me, and that will be a double good fortune; first, that my rival is cheated; next, that I shall be master of the lady's riches.

MAN. Doth your Worship mean the old lady?

DOCTOR. Who should I mean else?

MAN. Sir, she was married last night, about one of the clock, as her servant told me this morning.

DOCTOR. Married! to whom?

MAN. To a young Cavalier, one Mr. Dick Traveller.

DOCTOR. What the devil, hath he married her?

MAN. I know not whether the devil married them, but certainly they are married.

DOCTOR. Why, he is older than I.

MAN. He hath passed for a young man with the lady.

Enter another Man.

2 MAN. Sir, there's a young gentlewoman desires to speak with your Worship.

DOCTOR. 'Tis some comfort to converse with a young woman, after the loss of an old ——

The Doctor goes forth, and enters leading Mrs. Anne Sensible.

DOCTOR. Lady, wherein may I serve you?

ANNE. Sir, I am to desire your assistance for the cure of a disease I am troubled with.

DOCTOR. What disease?

ANNE. The disease of love.

DOCTOR. Truly, lady, a physician hath no remedy for that disease, unless the party be in love with the physician.

ANNE. The truth is, sir, I am in love with you.

DOCTOR. With me lady!

Enter [Harry] Sensible, and when he enters, he sees his sister, he starts back and frowns, she seems to be afraid.

HARRY. Are the Doctor and you so well acquainted, as you two to be private alone.

ANNE. Truly I was never here before.

HARRY. 'Tis false.

DOCTOR. I will assure you, Mr. Sensible, she speaks truth, for she was never here to my knowledge before.

HARRY. I perceive you both agree in a story, and I take it as an affront you should entertain my sister in private.

DOCTOR. I vow to Heaven I never saw her before this time, nor knew I that you were her brother.

HARRY. This answer will not serve me, for I will have satisfaction; and as for you, sister, I will offer you up as a sacrifice to honour.

He draws his sword, she shrieks out, and runs behind the Doctor,
the Doctor strives to defend her.

DOCTOR.   Sir, 'tis unworthy to draw your sword upon a woman, or to fight with an unarmed man.

HARRY.   I do not intend to fight with you at this time, but to kill my sister.

DOCTOR.   For what?

HARRY.   For visiting a man, and being alone with him in his chamber.

DOCTOR.   Why is that such a crime?

HARRY.   'Tis such a crime, that unless she can prove she is married, or assured, I will kill her.

ANNE.   Good Doctor save my life.

DOCTOR.   Then sir, give me leave to tell you, we are agreed to marry, may we have your consent?

HARRY.   I must have time to ask the advice of some dear friends first.

ANNE.   Dear brother consent, without advice.

HARRY.   That I will not.

ANNE.   Then send for your friends hither.

HARRY.   I have nobody here to send.

DOCTOR.   You may have two or three of my servants if you please.

Enter a Man.

MAN.   There are two gentlemen below that desire to speak with Mr. Sensible.

HARRY.   They are come as I desired, pray bring them in.

Enter Will Fullwit, and the Captain.

[HARRY]   Dear Will, and Captain, I was sending for you both, to ask your advice about a cause that hath much troubled me, which is a great concern[1] both to my justice and honour.

WILL.   What is that?

HARRY.   I coming to see Doctor Cure-all, found my sister out of my house, discoursing here alone with the Doctor, which is a great discredit for a young virgin, to be not only abroad without attendance, but in company with a man alone, and in his chamber.

CAPTAIN.   That is not well, I did not believe Mrs. Anne Sensible would have done such an act.

DOCTOR.   Gentlemen, the lady is not in fault, for she and I are agreed to marry, if her brother consents.

WILL.   That is another case; and will not you give your consent Harry?

HARRY.   I cannot tell.

CAPTAIN.   Come, come, you shall consent.

WILL.   Yes, yes, you shall Harry; Doctor give me your hand, and Mrs. Sensible give me yours, so join them together; do you agree truly and really to marry?

BOTH ANSWER.   We do.

CAPTAIN.   Then, Mr. Sensible, give them joy of their contract.

HARRY.   I wish you both joy.

Enter to the Doctor, Mrs. Peg Valorosa, Get-all, Sergeant Plead-all, and Mrs. Jane Fullwit.

GET-ALL.   Come, come, Captain Valorous, let us go to the church, for I am impatient.

SERGEANT.   Not so impatient as I.

CAPTAIN.   Faith, we come in here but to take another couple along with us.

GET-ALL.   Are they agreed?

HARRY.   They are, they are; there only wants that ceremony, you do, and all is sure.

Enter Dick Traveller, Lieutenant and Cornet.

---

1   concern] concernment F1

DICK. I am come only to make one to fill up the matrimonial triumphs.

HARRY. How doth my old lady like the young blade?

DICK. So well, as she is so well pleased, as it hath made her
half young again.

Enter Mistress Informer.

DICK. Welcome, Mrs. Informer.

INFORMER. By my troth, my heart did tremble, for fear I
should not come time enough to these fortunate nuptials.

GET-ALL. Well, to let all this company see, that I the first
deceived, am as well, if not better, pleased than the
deceivers; here I do promise to give my brother, that must
be Captain Valorous, twenty thousand pounds to maintain
his bastards, to discharge his whores, and to marry a virtuous and honourable wife; also, I give Doctor Feel-pulse,
Will Fullwit, five thousand pounds; and Harry Sensible five
thousand more; and five thousand pounds to the Lieutenant; and five thousand pounds between the Cornet and
Mrs. Informer; as for my judge Dick Traveller, I did intend
to have fee'd him well, and to give him money to have
bought a place in the Arches,[1] but he is better provided.

SERGEANT. I cannot present the whole society, but I will
make my brother Fullwit's five thousand pounds, you gave
him, ten.

DOCTOR. So will I give as much to my brother Harry Sensible.

DICK. And I will present the rest of the society.

WILL. Let's go unto church to make all sure,
For nothing in extremes will long endure.

CAPTAIN. Stay we must go to the hearing of my cousin Prudence's cause first, and then we shall have another couple.

[Exeunt]

---

1 Arches] The Court of Arches (or Arches for short) was the ecclesiastical court of
appeal for the province of Canterbury, once held at the Church of St-Mary-le-Bow
(or "of the Arches"), so called because of the arches that supported its steeple.

SCENE III

*The scene is a public hall, or pleading-court, wherein is a public
assembly, the young suitors and some other gallants,
taking one bar, and the young lady and her old suitor
another; and all bridal couples.*

One of the young suitors speaks.

[SUITOR] Most noble auditors.

I am chosen by my fellow-sufferers to declare the injustice
and injury this young lady has done us, and herself, by
refusing us that are young, handsome, healthy and strong,
for an old, infirm, weak and decayed man, who has neither
a clear eye-sight to admire her beauty, nor a perfect hearing
to be informed of her will; nor sufficient strength to fight
in her behalf, or defend her honour; nor that heat of affection that he can love her as she deserves. Indeed, it is not to
be suffered that old men and women should marry young
persons; for it is as much as to tie or bind the living and
dead together; for, though it cannot be truly said, that old
age is dead, yet we may say, 'tis rotten, and corruption is
next to death; for all creatures corrupt before they dissolve;
and we are taught by our holy fathers, that we must put off
the old man, and put on the new man : wherefore, 'tis not
lawful for this young lady to marry that old man, it being
both against Church and State, as not profitable to either,
but disadvantageous to both.

The Lady's Answer.

[PRUDENCE] Most noble auditors,

I come not here to express either my wit or malice, but to
defend my honest cause, and to express my true love;
wherefore, I shall briefly answer this gentleman's objections: first, as for the injustice he accuses me of, I utterly
deny that I am guilty, for to make a lawful choice is no
injustice to them; and to refuse a young man before an old

and wise one, is no injury to myself; next, what he says of their handsomeness, health and strength; I answer, that in my opinion, a handsome man is an error in nature, and health and strength are very uncertain in young men, for their vices decay one; and impair the other, before their natural time; whereas, the infirmities of old age are natural, neither infectious, unwholesome or dangerous to their wives: and though ancient men have not their hearing so quick, nor their eyesight so clear as young men, yet have they quicker wits, and clearer understandings, acquired by long experience of all sorts of actions, humors, customs, discourses, accidents, and fortunes amongst mankind; wherefore, old men cannot choose but be more knowing, rational and wise than young. Concerning the Church and State, since they do allow of buying and selling young maids to men to be their wives, they cannot condemn those maids that make their bargain to their own advantage, and choose rather to be bought than sold, and I confess I am one of the number of those; for I'll rather choose an old man that buys me with his wealth, than a young one, whom I must purchase with my wealth; who, after he has wasted my estate, may sell me to misery and poverty. Wherefore, our sex may well pray, from young men's ignorance and follies, from their pride, vanity and prodigality, their gaming, quarrelling, drinking and whoring, their pocky and diseased bodies, their mortgages, debts, and sergeants, their whores and bastards, and from all such sorts of vices and miseries that are frequent amongst young men, good Lord deliver us. But for fear of such a misfortune as to be a wife to a young man, I will marry this ancient man, and so, cousins, I am, if you please, ready to wait on you in church.

FINIS.

EPILOGUE

The Sociable Companions we hope do fit
Your judgments, fancies, and your wit:
This lady is ambitious, I dare say,
That all her hope is, that you'll like her play.
Which favour, she esteems at a high rate,
'Bove title, riches, or what's Fortune's fate;
She listens, with a trembling ear; she stands
Hoping to hear her joy, by your glad hands.

Appendix A: Selections from Margaret Cavendish's Autobiography

[Cavendish, Margaret. *A True Relation of my Birth, Breeding and Life*, as appended to *Natures Pictures Drawn by Fancies Pencil to the Life* (London, 1656), pp. 373-6, 383-91. The transcription here is taken from the British Library copy, which contains marginal corrections in Cavendish's own hand.]

...[W]hen the Queen was in Oxford, I had a great desire to be one of her maids of honour, hearing the Queen had not the same number she was used to have, whereupon I wooed and won my mother to let me go, for my mother being fond of all her children, was desirous to please them, which made her consent to my request: But my brothers and sisters seemed not very well pleased, by reason I had never been from home, nor seldom out of their sight; for though they knew I would not behave myself to their, or my own dishonour, yet they thought I might to my disadvantage, being unexperienced in the world, which indeed I did, for I was so bashful when I was out of my mother's, brothers', and sisters' sight, whose presence used to give me confidence, thinking I could not do amiss whilst any one of them were by, for I knew they would gently reform me if I did; besides, I was ambitious they should approve of my actions and behaviour, that when I was gone from them I was like one that had no foundation to stand, or guide to direct me, which made me afraid, lest I should wander with ignorance out of the ways of honour, so that I knew not how to behave myself. Besides, I had heard the world was apt to lay aspersions even on the innocent, for which I durst neither look up with my eyes, nor speak, nor be in any way sociable, insomuch as I was thought a natural fool, indeed I had not much wit, yet I was not an idiot, my wit was according to my years; and though I might have learnt more wit, and advanced my understanding by living in a court, yet being dull, fearful, and bashful, I neither heeded what was said or practised, but just what belonged to my loyal duty, and my own honest reputation; and indeed I was so afraid to dishonour my friends and family by my indiscreet actions, that I rather chose to be accounted a fool, than to be thought rude or wanton…. [F]or my lord the Marquis of Newcastle did approve of those bashful fears which many condemned, and would choose such a wife as he might bring to his own humours, and not such an one as was wedded to self-conceit, or one that had been tempered to the humours of another, for which he wooed me for his wife; and though I did dread marriage, and shunned men's companies, as much as I could, yet I could not, nor had not the power to refuse him, by reason my affections were fixed on him, and he was the only person I ever was in love with: Neither was I ashamed to own it, but gloried therein, for it was not amorous love, I never was infected therewith, it is a disease, or a passion, or both, I only know by relation, not by experience; neither could title, wealth, power or person entice me to love; but my love was honest and honourable, being placed upon merit, which affection joyed at the fame of his worth, pleased with delight in his wit, proud of the respects he used to me, and triumphing in the affections he professed for me, which affections he hath confirmed to me by a deed of time, sealed by constancy, and assigned by an unalterable decree of his promise, which makes me happy in despite of Fortune's frowns; for though misfortunes may and do oft dissolve base, wild, loose, and ungrounded affections, yet she hath no power of those that are united either by merit, justice, gratitude, duty, fidelity, or the like; and though my lord hath lost his estate, and banished out of his country for his loyalty to his King and country, yet neither despised poverty nor pinching necessity could make him break the bonds of friendship, or weaken his loyal duty to his King or country.

But not only the family I am linked to is ruined, but the family from which I sprung, by these unhappy wars, which ruin my mother lived to see, and then died, having lived a widow many years, for she never forgot my father so as to marry again; indeed he remained so lively in her memory, and her grief was so lasting, as she never mentioned his name, though she spoke often of him, but love and grief caused tears to flow, and tender sighs to rise, mourning in sad complaints; she made her house her cloister, enclosing herself, as it were therein, for she seldom went abroad, unless to church, but these unhappy wars forced her out, by reason she and her children were loyal to the King, for which they plundered her, and my brothers of all their goods, plate, jewels, money, corn, cattle, and the like, cut down their woods, pulled down their houses, and sequestered them from their lands and livings....

...[B]ut howsoever our fortunes are, we are both content, spending our time harmlessly, for my lord pleases himself with the management of some few horses, and exercises himself with the use of the sword; which two arts he hath brought by his studious thoughts, rational experience, and industrious practice to an absolute perfection: and though he hath taken as much pains in those arts, both by study and practice, as chemists, for the philosopher's stone, yet he hath this advantage of them, that he hath found the right and the truth thereof and therein, which chemists never found in their art, and I believe never will: also he recreates himself with his pen, writing what his wit dictates to him, but I pass my time rather with scribbling than writing, with words than wit, not that I speak much, because I am addicted to contemplation, unless I am with my lord, yet then I rather attentively listen to what he says, than impertinently speak, yet when I am writing any sad feigned stories, or serious humours or melancholy passions, I am forced many times to express them with the tongue before I can write them with the pen, by reason those thoughts that are sad, serious and melancholy, are apt to contract and to draw too much back, which oppression doth as it were overpower or smother the conception in the brain, but when some of those thoughts are sent out in words, they give the rest more liberty to place themselves, in a more methodical order, marching more regularly with my pen, on the ground of white paper, but my letters seem rather as a ragged rout, than a well-armed body, for the brain being quicker in creating, than the hand in writing, or the memory in retaining, many fancies are lost, by reason they oft-times outrun the pen, where I, to keep speed in the race, write so fast as I stay not so long as to write my letters plain, insomuch as some have taken my handwriting for some strange character, and being accustomed so to do: I cannot now write very plain, when I strive to write my best, indeed my ordinary handwriting is so bad as few can read it, so as to write it fair for the press, but however that little wit I have, it delights me to scribble it out, and disperse it about, for I being addicted from my childhood, to contemplation rather than conversation, to solitariness rather than society, to melancholy rather than mirth, to write with the pen than to work with a needle, passing my time with harmless fancies, their company

being pleasing, their conversation innocent, in which I take such pleasure, as I neglect my health, for it is as great a grief to leave their society, as a joy to be in their company, my only trouble is, lest my brain
should grow barren, or that the root of my fancies should become
insipid, withering into a dull stupidity for want of maturing subjects
to write on....

But now I have declared to my readers, my birth, breeding and
actions, to this part of my life, I mean the material parts, for should I
write every particular, as my childish sports and the like, it would be
ridiculous and tedious; but I have been honourably born and nobly
matched, my life hath been ruled with honesty, attended by modesty
and directed by truth: but since I have writ in general thus far of my
life, I think it fit, I should speak something of my humour, particular
practice and disposition....[A]s for my practice, I was never very
active, by reason I was given so much to contemplation; besides my
brothers and sisters, were for the most part serious, and staid in their
actions, not given to sport nor play, nor dance about, whose company
I keeping, made me so too: but I observed that although their actions
were staid, yet they would be very merry amongst themselves,
delighting in each others' company: also they would in their discourse
express the general actions of the world, judging, condemning,
approving, commending, as they thought good, and with those that
were innocently harmless, they would make themselves merry therewith; as for my study of books it was little, yet I chose rather to read,
than to employ my time in any other work, or practice, and when I
read what I understood not, I would ask my brother the Lord Lucas,
he being learned, the sense or meaning thereof, but my serious study
could not be much, by reason I took great delight in attiring, fine
dressing and fashions, especially such fashions as I did invent myself,
not taking that pleasure in such fashions as was invented by others:
also I did dislike anyone should follow my fashions, for I always took
delight in a singularity, even in accoutrements of habits, but whatsoever I was addicted to, either in fashions of cloths, contemplation of
thoughts, actions of life, they were lawful, honest, honourable and
modest, of which I can avouch to the world with a great confidence,
because it is a pure truth.
    ...I am a great emulator; for though I wish none worse than they
are, nor fear any should be better than they are, yet it is lawful for me

to wish myself the best and to do my honest endeavour thereunto, for I think it no crime to wish myself the exactest of nature's works, my thread of life the longest, my chain of destiny the strongest, my mind the peaceablest; my life the pleasantest, my death the easiest, and the greatest saint in heaven; also to do my endeavour, so far as honour and honesty doth allow of, to be the highest on Fortune's wheel, and to hold the wheel from turning, if I can, and if it be commendable to wish another's good, it were a sin not to wish my own; for as envy is a vice, so emulation is a virtue, but emulation is in the way to ambition, or indeed it is a noble ambition, but I fear my ambition inclines to vainglory, for I am very ambitious, yet 'tis neither for beauty, wit, titles, wealth or power, but as they are steps to raise me to Fame's tower, which is to live by remembrance in after-ages....[F]or perceiving the world is given, or apt to honour the outside more than the inside, worshipping show more than substance; and I am so vain, if it be a vanity, as to endeavour to be worshipped, rather than not to be regarded; yet I shall never be so prodigal as to impoverish my friends, or go beyond the limits or facility of our estate, and though I desire to appear at the best advantage, whilst I live in the view of the public world, yet I could most willingly exclude myself, so as never to see the face of any creature, but my lord, as long as I live, enclosing myself like an anchorite, wearing a frieze-gown tied with a cord about my waist: but I hope my readers, will not think me vain for writing my life, since there have been many that have done the like, as Caesar, Ovid, and many more, both men and women, and I know no reason I may not do it as well as they: but I verily believe some censuring readers will scornfully say, why hath this lady writ her own life? Since none cares to know whose daughter she was, or whose wife she is, or how she was bred, or what fortunes she had, or how she lived, or what humour or disposition she was of? I answer that it is true, that 'tis no purpose, to the readers, but it is to the authoress, because I write it for my own sake, not theirs; neither did I intend this piece for to delight, but to divulge, not to please the fancy, but to tell the truth, lest after-ages should mistake, in not knowing I was daughter to one Master Lucas of St. John's near Colchester in Essex, second wife to the Lord Marquis of Newcastle, for my lord having had two wives, I might easily have been mistaken, especially if I should die, and my lord marry again.

Appendix B: The Purposes of Plays: Selections from Prefaces to Playes (1662)

[From *Playes Written by the Thrice Noble, Illustrious, and Excellent Princess, the Lady Marchioness of Newcastle* (London, 1662), sigs. A3v, A7, A8.]

TO THE READERS

Noble Readers,

The reason why I put out my plays in print, before they are acted, is, first, that I know not when they will be acted, by reason they are in English, and England doth not permit, I will not say of wit, yet not of plays; and if they should, yet by reason all those that have been bred and brought up to act, are dead, or dispersed, and it would be an act of some time, not only to breed and teach some youths to act, but it will require some time to prove whether they be good actors or no; for if they are not bred to it whilst they be young, they will never be good actors when they are grown up to be men; for although someone by chance may have naturally, a facility to action, and a volubility of speech, and a good memory to learn, and get the parts by heart, or rote, yet it is very unlikely, or indeed impossible, to get a whole company of good actors without being taught and brought up thereto; the other reason is, that most of my plays would seem tedious upon the stage, by reason they are somewhat long, although most are divided into first and second parts; for having much variety in them, I could not possibly make them shorter, and being long, it might tire the spectators, who are forced, or bound by the rules of civility to sit out a play, if they be not sick; for to go away before a play is ended, is a kind of an affront, both to the poet and the players; yet, I believe none of my plays are so long as Ben Jonson's *Fox*, or *Alchemist*,[1] which in truth, are somewhat too long; but for the readers, the length of the plays can be no trouble, nor inconvenience, because they may read as short or as long a time as they please, without any disrespect to the

---

1 Ben Jonson's *Fox*, or *Alchemist*] Refers to *Volpone; or the Fox* (1605-6) and *The Alchemist* (1610), two of Ben Jonson's most famous and popular plays.

writer; but some of my plays are short enough; but the printing of my plays spoils them forever to be acted; for what men are acquainted with, is despised, at least neglected; for the newness of plays, most commonly, takes the spectators, more than the wit, scenes, or plot, so that my plays would seem lame or tired in action, and dull to hearing on the stage, for which reason, I shall never desire they should be acted; but if they delight or please the readers, I shall have as much satisfaction as if I had the hands of applause from the spectators.

M.N.

TO THE READERS

Noble Readers,

I make no question but that my plays will be censured, and those censurers severe, but I hope not malicious; but they will perchance say that my plays are too serious, by reason there is no ridiculous jest in them, nor wanton love, nor impossibilities; also 'tis likely they will say that there are no plots, nor designs, nor subtle contrivances, and the like; I answer, that the chief plots of my plays were to employ my idle time, the designs to please and entertain my readers, and the contrivance was to join edifying profit and delight together, that my readers may neither lose their time, nor grow weary in the reading; but if they find my plays neither edifying, nor delightful, I shall be sorry; but if they find either, I shall be pleased, and if they find both, I shall much rejoice, that my time hath been employed to some good use.

M.N.

I must trouble my noble readers to write of one thing more, which is concerning the reading of plays; for plays must be read to the nature of those several humours, or passions, as are expressed by writing: for they must not read a scene as they would read a chapter; for scenes must be read as if they were spoke or acted. Indeed comedies should be read a mimic way, and the sound of their voice must be according to the sense of the scene; and as for tragedies, or tragic scenes, they must not be read in a puling whining voice, but in a sad serious voice, as deploring or complaining: but the truth is there are as few good readers as good writers; indeed an ill reader is, as great a disadvantage to wit as wit can have, unless it be ill acted, for then 'tis doubly disgraced, both in the voice and action, whereas in reading only the voice is employed; but when a play is well and skillfully read, the very sound of the voice that enters through the ears, doth present the actions to the eyes of the fancy as lively as if it were really acted; but howsoever writings must take their chance, and I leave my plays to Chance and Fortune, as well as to censure and reading.

M.N.

Appendix C: Warrior Women and Royalist Disorder: Letters from the Front

[From letters by Edward Norgate to Robert Reade, in *Calendar of State Papers Domestic 1639* (London: H.M. Stationery Office, 1858–1897): 144-6; 282-3.]

1. May 9, Newcastle — In my last I gave you intimation of the King's proclamation to the Covenanters, which was sent to Edinburgh by Sir James Carmichael, now a week past, of the event whereof we are in continual expectation, as thereon depends the good or ill of both kingdoms. This proclamation was read on Sunday last in the church here in the presence of the Lord General, the Earls of Essex, Holland, and other lords and commanders. Of these proclamations, the Marquis Hamilton, now riding at anchor near Leith, hath six, whereof he is to make use according as he shall hear it either accepted or refused, and we have brought hither a printer with all his trinkets ready to make new as occasion may require, because it seems the King will leave nothing unattempted nor any way of grace or means to express it untried, if possibly he can reclaim the worst of subjects to their due obedience.... They say the Marquis's mother, the old Lady Marchioness, hearing of her son's approach near the coast, animates all other ladies and gentlewomen to make all possible resistance, that they in person work at the fort at Leith, carrying earth and stones, refusing no labour to make good the place against their Sovereign; that this lady came forth armed with a pistol, which she vowed to discharge upon her own son, if he offered to come ashore — a notable virago!...The unwelcome news has come of the refusal of the King's proclamation,[1] which they say is unconditional and unsure, with which the King is, as well he may be, justly displeased. What we shall do or suffer God knows; but it is thought the King will on, and no longer suffer so intolerable insolency. Nothing here is so false and detested as a Scotch Covenanter. What counsels now we shall fall

---

1 Proclamation] Refers to King Charles I's doomed attempt to impose English liturgy in Scotland by royal decree in 1637.

upon God knows; hence we must on Wednesday next, the King to his tents and those that have any, the rest be endued[1] with patience instead of a rug-gown.... My money is almost gone, and my next work must be to send to my associates present and to come for fresh supplies. In good earnest all is naught, and I pray God this be not the beginning of our miseries, for here is great distraction. Commend me to my brother Warwick, and say that in Cranfield's[2] time, who loved nobody I got payment of 200l. out of the Exchequer. If in this man's reign, beloved and loving all folks, I can get nothing, it is a sad story.

2. June 5, Berwick — Here is great talk of my old lady, Marchioness of Hamilton; of her case of pistols at her saddle, for she leads her own troop of horse, and is in the field, and her case of dags[3] at her girdle. Her silver bullets are not forgotten for her own son and my Lord General, and how the ladies and gentlewomen, by her example, do all practice their arms, in which a new kind of housewifery they are very expert. Of the form of their, I mean the women's, imprecation and curse, every one talks, and certainly but too true, wishing their husband's and children's flesh to be converted into that of dogs, and their souls annihilated, is the word, or damned the meaning, if they refuse to come into the covenant, or ever consent to admit of the bishops; of the reason of which total defection and fell rage against these men, though no reason can be given, yet I verily believe, and so do many others, that no man alive can hope to see the restoration of the men or order, without a final extermination and destruction of all. They say that in their camp they have daily prayers and weekly fasts, praying for the King, &c.... And I pray God the begun dislikes of some great men here against some other greater, grow not into a foolish faction, to the King's disservice and prejudice of the business. I was told last night, by a person of honour, that the Earl of Newcastle desired to know of the General of the Horse where he should march, and was assigned the rear. The Earl thinks himself wronged, both in respect of his gallant troop, being six score of the best horse, and men of best

---

1 endued] covered by, clad in.
2 Cranfield] Sir Lionel Cranfield, Earl of Middlesex and Lord Treasurer during James I's reign, brought down by impeachment in 1624 a year before the succession of Charles I.
3 dags] a kind of heavy pistol or hand-gun.

estates in the army, as also in respect of their title, being called the Prince's troop, and indeed he bears, by permission of the Prince, his arms of three feathers in his cornet. The Earl of Holland[1] sends word, as my relator says, that he could take no notice it was the Prince's troop but by a borrowed name or so. The Earl of Newcastle, not willing to contest, complies with the General's command, and marches where he was appointed, but takes off the Prince's arms from the lance and goes without a cornet.[2] This, at last, comes to the King, who orders the Earl's troop to march in the first place next his own. Of this and the like stuff I fear we shall hear more than enough.

[From a letter by Lieutenant-Colonel Roger Sawrey to William Clarke, reprinted in *Report on the Manuscripts of F.W. Leyborne-Popham, Esq.* Historical Manuscripts Commission. (Norwich, 1899): 112.]

3. 1657, April 6. Citadel at Ayr—I with my company got very well to Ayr upon Saturday, where we found all things in good order and friends in health, only a young person with Captain-Lieutenant Shockly, entertained the last muster, who is since discovered to be a woman; her name she saith is Ann Dimack, daughter to one John Dimack of Keale, near Bullingbrooke Castle in Lincolnshire. She hath been with us but one muster, and saith that her father and mother being dead she lived with her aunt, and fell in love with one John Evison, who had served his time in London, but was a Lincolnshire man. Her friends were against it, and would by no means yield to their marriage, nor had she any way of accomplishing her end left, but by putting herself into a man's habit, which she did in May, 1655, and so [they] went to London together, and finding him not to be in a capacity to live they both resolved to betake themselves to service, this maid still keeping in man's apparel, and went as two brothers. The young man lived at Islington, and the maid at London with a coach man in Chick Lane, whose name was Taylor, where she served

---

1 Earl of Holland] King Charles's General of Horse, and thus in charge of cavalry and troop deployments. William Cavendish had a passionate interest in horsemanship, publishing a lavish book expounding his own theories and methods on the subject (*La Méthode Nouvelle et Invention Extraordinaire de dresser les Chevaux*) in 1658.
2 cornet] the standard of a troop of cavalry.

two years under the name of Stephen Evison, and after that coming with John by sea the said John was cast away, and she, keeping still her man's habit, came to Carlisle, and there listed herself for a soldier under Major Tollhurst by the name of John Evison, and there she continued until she came to this garrison, and never was known to any, which she declares very solemnly to be all the way of her progress in her disguise. And I can perceive nothing but modesty in her carriage since she hath been with us, and shall send to the other places where she hath been formerly to know the truth of her declaration. If you think it necessary you may acquaint my Lord General with it, with my respects to yourself and lady, returning you hearty thanks for your late kindness.

Appendix D: Warrior Women: The Queen and the War

[Green, Mary Anne Everett, ed. *Letters of Queen Henrietta Maria, Including her Private Correspondence with Charles the First.* London: Richard Bentley, 1857. p. 200, 222.]

1. York, May 14 1643

...I hope now that the ammunition is arrived, you may stay at Oxford, on the defensive, till I can arrive; and to this effect, I have sent Jermyn to Lord Newcastle, to press him to give me nine hundred men, who are coming from Newcastle and Berwick, that have no arms. If that succeed, I doubt not of bringing you four thousand men well provided with the equipments of a little army, in spite of all the hindrances there are, which are not small, for our general and all the gentlemen of the country are against it. This army is called the Queen's army, but I have little power over it, and I assure you that if I had, all would go on better than it does.

2. Newark, June 27 1643

...At this present, I think it fit to let you know the state in which we march, and what I leave behind me for the safety of Lincolnshire and Nottinghamshire: I leave two thousand foot, and wherewithal to arm five hundred more, and twenty companies of horse; all this to be under Charles Cavendish, whom the gentlemen of the country have desired me not to carry with me—against his will, for he desired extremely to go. The enemies have left within Nottingham one thousand. I carry with me three thousand foot, thirty companies of horse and dragoons, six pieces of cannon, and two mortars. Harry Jemyn commands the forces which go with me, as colonel of my guards, and Sir Alexander Lesly the foot under him, and Gerard the horse, and Robin Legg the artillery, and her she-majesty generalissima, and extremely diligent, with one hundred and fifty wagons of baggage to govern, in case of battle.

[Motteville, Madame Françoise de. *Memoirs for the History of Anne of Austria*.... *Translated from the original French*. 5 vols. London, 1726. Vol. I, p.219-21.]

3. [Jan.-Feb.1643] After this Princess [Queen Henrietta Maria] had rested about a fortnight, she courageously put to sea with nine ships that were left, for two of them were lost; and this bout she landed safely in England at a little village on the seaside. There she stayed some days expecting troops from the King to receive and escort her. The Parliament's forces, that had followed close at her heels, and which had pursued her by sea, coasted along by the very place where she lay; and as she was asleep in bed, she was awakened by the enemy's cannon-shot, which went through the cottage where she lay. My Lord Germain, her chief Gentleman of the Querry, and Minister, came to wait upon her, and told her she was in such imminent danger, that there was an absolute necessity for her escaping. Accordingly, she left the place, after putting on a gown, and went to conceal herself in the caves without the village. She had an ugly lap-dog, named Mitte, which she was very fond of; and remembering in the middle of the village, that she had left Mitte asleep in her bed, she returned the way she came, and not fearing her pursuers, she brought away her favourite, and then retired as fast as she could from cannon-shot. When the Parliamentarians were weary with cannonading, and the King's troops were arrived, the Queen set out to meet him. She augmented his troops with some levies which she made in that county, and furnished them with arms that she brought over with her. Having mustered a gallant army, she put herself at the head of it, and marched on directly towards the King her husband, always riding on horseback without the effeminacy of a woman, and living with her soldiers in the manner that it may be imagined Alexander did with his. She ate with them in the open field without any ceremonies. She treated them as brethren, and they all loved her entirely. These were moderate victories, and he that conquered all Asia, ran more hazards, fought more battles, and made more conquests than this Princess. Hers was to take a town in the road, which...was considerable and of importance to her service. The King her husband received her with joy, being ravished with her courage and affection; and when they saw

what fine troops they had, they hoped to bear down their rebellious faithless subjects; but all their forces dispersed soon after, and proved to be of no service to them.

Appendix E: Marriage Markets: Selections from Margaret Cavendish's Sociable Letters

[From Margaret Cavendish, *CCXI Sociable Letters* (London, 1664): pp. 18-20, 48-51, 82-83, 100-103, 295-6.]

1. Letter 13

Madam,

Most of Mrs. L.A.'s discourse is of herself, indeed everyone is apt to speak of himself, as being full of self-love, which makes most tongues discourse of a self-theme; but her theme, is to tell how good a wife she will make when she is married, although the proof will be after she is married, if she can get a husband; for I believe she wants one, and desires one, because she talks so much of a husband, and promises so well for a husband. Truly, it is to be observed, that all maids love to talk of husbands, all widows of suitors, and all wives of lovers: for men may marry, nay do often marry, yet not for love, but for interest as for posterity,[1] or the like; and suitors may woo, yet not for love, but interest, as for wealth, or the like; But when amorous lovers plead, it is for no other design but to lie with the woman they make their address to; and married wives are more apt to yield than maids or widows, having a cloak to cover their shame or reproach, and a husband to father their children; and they are more fond of amorous courtships than maids or widows, because they are more barr'd, as being bound in wedlock's bonds: besides, it requires more secrecy and difficulty; both [of] which women love. But when maids, widows, and wives talk of husbands, suitors, and lovers, they are so delighted with the discourse, as you may perceive, not only by their speech, being then quicker, and their wit sharper, and words fluenter, but also by their looks, their eyes being livelier, their countenances pleasanter, and their behaviour gayer or wantoner, than in any other discourse, especially if it be upon particular persons, such as they fancy, or think they fancy them. But as for Mrs. L.A. who discourses so much of a husband, I do verily believe, she will make a very good wife, not that she says so, but that

---

1 as for posterity] such as to produce children.

she hath been bred strictly and retiredly, and is of a sober, and stay'd nature, not apt to run into extravagancies, nor to desire variety of company, but is huswifly and thrifty, and of an humble and obedient behaviour, and not only attentive to good advices, but tractable and practive[1] to them; all which makes her deserve a good husband, and I wish her one with all my heart; but she must take her fortune, whether none or any, bad or good; but many a good bachelor makes an ill husband, and many a wild debauched bachelor makes a good husband; and as for widowers, many men that were good husbands to their first wives, are ill husbands to their second, or third, or fourth, or to some good, and some bad; and some that have been ill and unkind husbands to their first wives, are very good, and fond husbands to their second: the like for maids, wives and widows; so as none can make a wise choice in haphazard; for haphazard, as chance, bars out wisdom's prudence, it blindfolds wisdom, having no sunlight into chance; so as a fool blinded with ignorance, may choose in the lottery of husbands and wives, as well as the wisest, being blinded with the inconstancy of mankind. But leaving Mrs. L.A. to the lottery, and her matrimonial contemplations and discourses, I rest,

Madam,

Your faithful friend and servant.

2. Letter 26

Madam,

We have no news here, unless to hear that the Lady C.R. did beat her husband, and because she would have witness enough, she beat him in a public assembly, nay, being a woman of none of the least sizes, but one of the largest, and having anger added to her strength, she did beat him soundly, and it is said that he did not resist her, but endured it patiently; whether he did it out of fear to show his own weakness, being not able to encounter her, or out of a noble nature, not to strike a woman, I know not; yet I believe the best: and surely, if he doth not, or cannot tame her spirits, or bind her hands, or for love will not leave her, if she beat him often, he will have but a sore life. Indeed I was sorry when I heard of it, not only for the sake of our sex, but because she and he are persons of dignity, it belonging rather to mean born

---

1 practive] apt to practice.

and bred women to do such unnatural actions; for certainly, for a wife to strike her husband, is as much, if not more, as for a child to strike his father; besides, it is a breach of matrimonial government, not to obey all their husbands' commands; but those women that strike or cuckold their husbands are matrimonial traitors, for which they ought to be highly punished; as for blows, they ought to be banished from their husband's bed, house, [and] family, and for adultery they ought to suffer death, and their executioner ought to be their husband. 'Tis true, passion will cause great indiscretion, and women are subject to violent passions, which make or cause them so often to err in words and actions, which, when their passion is over, they are sorry for; but unruly passions are only a cause of uncivil words and rude actions, whereas adultery is caused by unruly appetites; wherefore women should be instructed and taught more industriously, carefully, and prudently to temper their passions, and govern their appetites, than men, because there comes more dishonour from their unruly passions and appetites than from men's; but for the most part women are not educated as they should be, I mean those of quality, for their education is only to dance, sing, and fiddle, to write complimental[1] letters, to read romances, to speak some language that is not their native, which education, is an education of the body, and not of the mind, and shows that their parents take more care of their feet than their head, more of their words than of their reason, more of their music than their virtue, more of their beauty than their honesty, which methinks is strange, as that their friends and parents should take more care, and be at greater charge to adorn their bodies, than to endue their minds, to teach their bodies arts, and not to instruct their minds with understanding; for this education is more for outward show, than for inward worth, it makes the body a courtier, and the mind a clown, and sometimes it makes their body a bawd, and their mind a courtesan, for though the body procures lovers, yet it is the mind that is the adultress, for if the mind were honest and pure, they would never be guilty of that crime; wherefore those women are best bred, whose minds are civilest as being well taught and govern'd, for the mind will be wild and barbarous, unless it be enclosed with study, instructed by learning, and governed by knowledge and understanding, for then the inhabitants

---

1 complimental] full of compliments.

of the mind will live peaceably, happily, honestly, and honourably, by which they will rule and govern their associate appetites with ease and regularity, and their words, as their household servants, will be employed profitably. But leaving the Lady C.R. and her husband to passion and patience, I rest,

Madam,

Your faithful friend and servant.

3. Letter 39

Madam,

I may give the Lady F.L. joy of her second marriage, for I hear she is married again; but I fear it will be applied to her, what is said of another Lady, who married first very well for title and wealth, her husband being in years, but she very poor, and amongst much company it was told, she seem'd to be a crafty, witty woman, that she could get such an husband; no, said one man, it was not the wit or craft of the lady that got her such a husband, but the folly of the man that married such a wife; and after he died and left her very rich, she married a young man that had no estate, and then they said that it seem'd her second husband was a wise man, that he could get so rich a wife; no, said the former man, it was not the wisdom of the man, but the folly of the woman, that caus'd that match; so she was even with her first husband in folly, for he play'd the fool to marry her, and she play'd the fool to marry her second husband. Thus most of the world of mankind is mistaken, for what they attribute to some men's wit, is other men's folly, but for marriages, the truth is, that folly makes more marriages than prudence; as for example, Mr. A.B. hath married a common courtesan, if she had been particular, it had been more excusable; but all men are not so foolish, for I hear that Sir W.S. will rather endure the persecution of his own courtesan, than marry her. But leaving the Lady F.L. to her new husband, and Mr. A.B. to his new wife, and Sir W.S. to his pursuing whore, I rest,

Madam,

Your faithful friend and servant.

4. Letter 50

Madam,

I cannot wonder that Mrs. F.G. is so desirous of a husband, for I observe, that all unmarried women, both maids and widows, are the like, insomuch that there are more customers that go to Hymen's markets, which are churches, plays, balls, masques, marriages, etc., than there are husbands to be sold, and all prices are bidden there, as beauty, birth, breeding, wit and virtue, though virtue is a coin whereof is not much; but husbands are so scarce, especially good ones, as they are at such great rates, that an indifferent price will not purchase any one, wherefore those that will buy them, must be so rich as to be able to bestow an extraordinary price of beauty, birth, breeding, wit or virtue, and yet much ado to purchase any one, nay, some cannot be had without all those join'd into one; but Venus's markets, which are also public meetings, (for all markets are public) are so well stor'd of all sorts and degrees of titles, professions, ages, and the like, as they are as cheap as stinking mackerel, and all coins are current there, but virtue, wherefore that is never offer'd; 'tis true, the markets of Hymen and Venus are in one and the same city or place, yet Hymen and Venus sell apart, like as several graziers[1] bring their Beasts to one market or fair; I call them several markets, to make a distinction of which belongs to Hymen, and which to Venus; but for better distinction's sake, I will put them into shops apart, or into as many pews in one church, or compare them to several scenes in one masque, several acts in one play, for as many stalls or shops there are in one market, and several magistrates in one city, so many shops have Hymen and Venus in one market; but the cheapest that are to be sold out of Hymen's shops, are young novices; and although there is much scarcity in Hymen's shops, yet the price of gold or such riches, if they be offer'd, buys any man that is there to be sold, which are bachelors and widowers, for there's no married man in Hymen's shops, unless unknown that they were bought before, and once discover'd, they are punish'd, for married men can neither be bought nor sold by Hymen or his customers, until they be widowers; but in Venus's shops there be as many, if not more, married men than bachelors or widowers; but both in Hymen and Venus's shops there are of all sorts, better and worse, [such]

---

1 graziers] those who feed cattle in preparation for market.